DATE DUE

Educating Students
on the Autistic Spectrum

Educating Students
on the Autistic Spectrum
A Practical Guide

Martin Hanbury

2nd
Edition

SAGE

Los Angeles | London | New Delhi
Singapore | Washington DC

First published 2012

SAGE Publications Ltd
1 Oliver's Yard
55 City Road
London EC1Y 1SP

SAGE Publications Inc.
2455 Teller Road
Thousand Oaks, California 91320

SAGE Publications India Pvt Ltd
B 1/I 1 Mohan Cooperative Industrial Area
Mathura Road
New Delhi 110 044

SAGE Publications Asia-Pacific Pte Ltd
3 Church Street
#10-04 Samsung Hub
Singapore 049483

Library of Congress Control Number: 2011929790

British Library Cataloguing in Publication data

A catalogue record for this book is available from the British Library

ISBN 978-0-85702-893-8
ISBN 978-0-85702-894-5 (pbk)

Typeset by C&M Digitals (P) Ltd, Chennai, India
Printed by CPI Antony Rowe, Chippenham, Wiltshire
Printed on paper from sustainable resources

Contents

Acknowledgements   vi

About the author   vii

Downloadable materials   viii

List of figures   ix

Introduction   1

1   Autism: an overview   3

   *Kanner and Asperger • Causation • Diagnosis • Prevalence • Models
   of autism • A changing context*

2   The impact of autism on learning   15

   *The effect of the condition • Behavioural issues: fear, flight
   and fight • Attitudes to autism*

3   Sharing positive attitudes towards students with autism   27

   *Working with Professionals • Nurturing home–school
   relationships • Peer relationships*

4   Addressing behavioural issues in autism   37

   Overcoming fear • Flight responses • Understanding violent behaviour

5   Understanding the effect of the condition   55

   *Social understanding in the classroom • Supporting communication
   • Developing flexible thinking • Supporting sensory processing*

6   Effective and established strategies   75

   Assessment • Interventions and approaches • Evaluation

7   Developing the curriculum for individuals with autism   95

   *Complexity and learning • Towards a new pedagogy • A structure
   for learning • The double helix curriculum model • Conclusion*

Epilogue   110

Appendix: INSET materials   111

References   122

Index   126

Acknowledgements

Those of us fortunate enough to work with children and young people learn something new each day. Generally, it is the youngster who leads our development as practitioners and our progress depends largely on our ability to respond to what we have learnt. I hope I have listened to those I have worked with and would like to thank them for all they have taught me. Equally, the families and carers of these children and young people are a special group of people. Their resilience, creativity and focus on their children's needs have been both inspirational and informative. Again, I would like to thank them all.

I have faced the challenges we all encounter in education alongside colleagues whose skill, expertise and commitment has deepened my faith in humankind. Many colleagues have supported the development of this second edition and I would like to thank especially Graham Birtwell, Jill Breden, Francine Brower, Debi Brown, Barry Carpenter, Keith Cox, Anne Murray, Tony Newman, Steve Pyott, Lisa Sharrock, Jim Taylor and Lucy Wood, for their positive attitudes towards this project.

Similarly, I have benefited enormously from the encouragement and advice of my editor, Jude Bowen. This second edition has provided me with the opportunity to explore this wonderful field in more depth; a gift I thank her for.

Finally, I must thank Theresa for coffee and cake, and Megan, Tim, Patrick and Fran for keeping the noise down – well sometimes!

About the author

Martin Hanbury is a Head Teacher and author who has worked in the field of autism for over 25 years in a variety of roles including carer, teaching assistant, teacher and, latterly, school leader.

Martin holds Master's degrees in Special Education, Educational Management and Research Methodology and a Doctorate in Educational Leadership. He has written *Educating Students on the Autistic Spectrum* (2005) and *Positive Behaviour Strategies to Support Children and Young People with Autism* (2007) for SAGE alongside a number of other chapters and articles related to special educational needs and autism. Martin is currently researching the accessibility of educational, health and social services for students with learning difficulties and disabilities.

Martin contributes to a number of university courses focused on autism, and delivers training in the field on a regular and frequent basis to a variety of agencies. Martin has been an active participant in the National Autistic Society's accreditation programme for many years.

Downloadable materials

This book is supported by a wealth of resources that can be downloaded from www.sagepub.co.uk/martinhanbury for use in your setting. A full list of the resources available is below:

Training PowerPoint Presentation 1

Training PowerPoint Presentation 2

Chapter 3

Figure 3.1   Observation checklist

Chapter 4

Figure 4.2   Flowchart for risk assessment

Figure 4.3   Needs checklist

Figure 4.8   Behaviour support plan

Chapter 5

Figure 5.1   Student profile

Chapter 7

Figure 7.3   Self-evaluation

Figures

1.1	The triad of impairment	9
2.1	Autism: three waves of impact	16
3.1	Observation checklist	29
4.1	Same challenge, different child	40
4.2	Flowchart for risk assessment	45
4.3	Needs checklist	49
4.4	Grading needs	50
4.5	Priority	50
4.6	Hierarchy	50
4.7	Proportion	50
4.8	Behaviour support plan	53
5.1	Student profile	57
5.2	Supporting communication: dos	67
5.3	Supporting communication: don'ts	67
6.1	Transition area	83
6.2	Schedules	85
7.1	Complexity theory and complex learners	97
7.2	Reflection: trans-disciplinary practice	99
7.3	Self-evaluation	103
7.4	The double helix curriculum model	104
7.5	Linking the strands	106
7.6	Planning template: English	106
7.7	Planning template: Mathematics	107
7.8	Planning template: Science	107
7.9	Holistic learning programme	108

Introduction

The field of autism is a dynamic, rapidly evolving world in which new ideas, fresh theories and innovative practices are continuously emerging in an apparently endless stream. In the time that has elapsed since the first edition of this book was published there have been a number of important developments which have fundamentally affected the lives and experiences of people with autism and moved forward thinking in the field exponentially. Advances in medical research such as the work of the Autism Genome Project, critical changes in the law embodied in The Autism Act of 2009 and an increasing awareness of the condition exemplified by the 2009 Inclusion Development Programme's focus on autism have all served to alter the landscape of autism for ever.

These changes have driven the evolution of whole life perspectives for people with autism underpinned by Temple Grandin's notion that 'Autism is a part of who I am'. This holistic view has enabled a paradigm shift away from the deficit model of autism in which we seek to ameliorate core characteristics towards an understanding of the condition which recognises the strengths, qualities and unique value of each individual. Crucially, this view enables a positive view of autism to emerge through which people are empowered and enriched.

This is not to say that people with autism do not experience significant challenges and difficulties in their lives. For example, the National Autistic Society (www.autism.org.uk) report that 40 per cent of children with autism have been bullied and that 50 per cent of students with autism have been excluded from school at some point. In adult life, only 15 per cent of people with autism have full-time permanent employment and over 30 percent of adults with autism experience some degree of mental health problem. Nor should we underestimate the potential scale of the issue with an estimated half a million people with autism living in the UK. which, when families are considered, entails that somewhere in the region of 2 million people every day have some contact with or experience of autism. Translating this into the school-aged population (Baird et al. 2006) indicates that the average primary school may have two or three students with autism on roll while an average secondary may expect somewhere between eight and ten students with autism in their population. With birth rates rapidly rising, we might reasonably assume that these figures will increase proportionately.

Therefore, we face a collective challenge in improving the quality of life of a significant number of people and can only hope to achieve this by ensuring that each component of an individual's life is addressed in a thorough and coherent manner. This requires people with autism, their parents and carers, practitioners in the field and commissioning bodies to work in close collaboration in order to create opportunities for enriching and fulfilling lives. In the past, where this co-operation has been secured, great advances have been made; where it has not, the quality of life for people with autism has suffered.

This new edition endeavours to incorporate the major changes in the field of autism into the original proposition of the book, that is, to provide a practical guide to support students with autism. While this core objective remains the same, there are new challenges emerging and therefore the need to revise and update the original text. For example, developments in our understanding of sensory processing difficulties are addressed at several key points in the book and approaches which support students with autism in this area are explored.

Similarly, the significant growth in the numbers of students with autism educated within the mainstream sector has prompted a major revision of part of the original text. The majority of students with autism are now educated in mainstream provision and educators need to ensure that we can provide a meaningful, learner-focused programme for each individual by developing our curriculum and our practice to meet an ever-changing need. The complexities of this challenge are considered at length in the Chapter 7 of this book along with a model for developing the curriculum to meet the needs of learners with autism in all settings.

For those of us living and working on a day-to-day basis in the field of autism there is a palpable sense of change and growth as practice becomes better informed and more refined. And yet there is a still a sense of so much that remains unknown and so much more for us to learn as we move forward. It is hoped that this new edition provides further impetus to that journey with fresh ideas and deeper insights into our collective understanding.

Finally, experience suggests that *answers* change with time and the tide; it is the *questions* which remain the same. As Einstein advised, the important thing is not to stop questioning.

1

Autism: an overview

This chapter:

- **Provides a brief history of autism including discussion of theories causation, diagnostic criteria and changes in prevalence**
- **Presents current understanding of the condition through the conceptual models of the triad of impairment, mind-blindness, difficulties in executive function, difficulties in central coherence and difficulties with processing sensory information**
- **Considers the rapidly changing field of autism**

Kanner and Asperger

It is in the seminal work of Leo Kanner (1943) that we first find the word autism applied to an identifiable group of youngsters who shared common characteristics representing a unique and specific condition separate to any other childhood conditions. A year later, Hans Asperger (1944) working in wartime Austria, reported a group of adolescents who, although of average or above average intelligence, shared the same features of social ineptitude, inflexible thought patterns and idiosyncratic use of language. In the immediate aftermath of war, it was Kanner's work which received wider publicity and engaged the scientific community in further studies of causation and definition.

Kanner's initial work focused on 11 children, eight boys and three girls, who at the time he was writing were all under the age of 11. Kanner identified in these children many of the features of autism we would recognise today including

- 'the inability to relate themselves in the ordinary way to people and situations'

- 'the absence of spontaneous sentence formation'

- 'insistence on sameness' (Kanner, 1943: 242–5 passim).

Moreover Kanner recognised that despite the variation among the individual children he was studying, there existed sufficient common characteristics to denote a specific condition. He says

> The eleven children (eight boys and three girls) whose histories have been briefly presented, offer, as is to be expected, individual differences in the degree of their disturbance, the manifestation of specific features, the family constellation, and the step-by-step development in the course of years. But even a quick review of the material makes the emergence of a number of essential common characteristics appear inevitable. These characteristics form a unique 'syndrome,' not heretofore reported, which seems to be rare enough, yet is probably more frequent than is indicated by the paucity of observed cases. (Kanner 1943: 241–2)

and, in articulating this notion of a singular condition comprised of a range of manifestations, Kanner prefigured the complexity of the condition which was to gradually emerge over the coming decades.

The circumstances of war entailed that Asperger remained unaware of Kanner's paper and use of the term 'autism' when publishing his own work. Asperger used the same label to describe four children aged between 6 and 11, who showed marked difficulties in social integration despite apparently adequate cognitive and verbal skills. Asperger drew a distinction between his patients' lack of social contact and the withdrawal of children with schizophrenia by highlighting the fact that children with schizophrenia displayed a progressive withdrawal whereas his patients showed this aloofness from the outset. Asperger (1944) stressed that difficulties with social interaction were the defining feature of his conditions but also provided a comprehensive list of symptoms and features, including:

- difficulties in interpreting non-verbal communication such as facial expressions and body movements

- peculiar use of language

- obsessive interests in narrowly defined areas

- clumsiness and poor body awareness

- behavioural problems

- familial and gender patterns.

In many respects Asperger's original work had little influence on the field of autism until the 1970s. Then, as notions about autism evolved to incorporate a broader spectrum (Gillberg 1985; Wing and Gould 1979), so the group associated with Asperger began to be included in the debate. Because of the distinctions between the two original groups studied, it became usual to describe people of lower cognitive ability as classically autistic, or as experiencing Kanner's autism, whereas more able individuals were seen as experiencing Asperger's Syndrome.

It is important to note at this point that the relationship between autism and Asperger's syndrome remains a controversial arena for discussion (Cohen and Volkmar 1997). The basic standpoints are:

- Kanner's autism and Asperger's Syndrome are part of a spectrum of associated conditions known as autistic spectrum conditions. People with Asperger's Syndrome represent a high-functioning group within the spectrum.

- Asperger's Syndrome is distinct from other conditions. High-functioning autism is not the same as Asperger's Syndrome; there are qualitative differences in the condition.

Studies which have attempted to identify criteria which discriminate between autism and Asperger's Syndrome have yielded mixed results. We must recognise that understanding of autism is still at a very early stage in its evolution and consensus over the precise demarcation of groups will remain problematic for some time to come. As educators, our primary concern does not lie with diagnostic distinctions but rather with the features of the condition(s) which adversely affect a student's ability to learn; our focus must remain here.

Causation

Early ideas of causation were obscure and confusing. It must be remembered that Kanner was a psychiatrist operating in the climate of psychoanalytic thinking which had come to dominate in the 1940s. Consequently, thinking around the cause of autism began to form around theories of parenting and in particular the role of the mother in nurturing the child. Fortunately, by the mid-1960s the work of Rimland (1964) and others demonstrated that autism had a biological basis and should be regarded in the same way as any other condition.

Today, the question of causation remains complex with research focused in three key areas, namely:

- psychology

- neurology

- genetics.

Each of these fields may be characterised as follows:

- Psychology – related to an individual's cognition, perception and understanding. Research has focused on language, memory, spatial awareness, sensory perception, social awareness, empathic awareness.

- Neurology – related to the dysfunction of particular structures of the brain and the neuro-chemicals which transmit information within the brain. The commonality of symptoms across the spectrum has led researchers to investigate a unique underlying neurobiology.

- Genetics – related to the inherent characteristics which make up an individual. The Autism Genome Project (AGP) has successfully identified a number of genetic locations associated with autism. Recent research from AGP indicates that scientists are moving towards an understanding of how each of these genetic factors interlink with one another.

While investigations in each of these key areas is essential for furthering our understanding of autism, the differing perspectives held by researchers in each discrete field can lead to confusion. Furthermore, definitions of the term 'cause' may vary significantly among researchers just as the phenomena being studied may be wide ranging. Consequently, there are a variety of different, sometimes conflicting, theories of causation.

For our purposes as educators, it is necessary to take a pragmatic view on this issue. Based on what we know, it is reasonable to see autism as *a behaviourally defined developmental condition resulting from neurological characteristics caused by genetic factors*.

If we ask 'what causes autism?' our answers lie along a complex chain of events defined by several levels of causation. A geneticist answering the question may refer to the locus of genetic events; a neurologist will reference brain pathologies determined by those events; and a psychologist will point to the developmental issues impacting on an individual as a consequence of their neurological make-up. Our understanding, as educators, is best informed by taking account of this complexity and attempting to integrate each level of causation in order to produce a picture of the whole child.

A further point to consider is that at each level there may be a number of possible causes. Therefore, there may be a *number* of genetic factors, a *variety* of possible brain pathologies and a *range* of developmental impairments which lead to the spectrum of behaviour we term autism. Indeed, the fact that there are perhaps many permutations of causation may well account for the breadth of the spectrum and the 'fascinating peculiarities' (Kanner 1943) of each unique individual with autism.

Diagnosis

In 1980 the American Psychiatric Association published the third edition of their *Diagnostic and Statistical Manual of Mental Conditions*, known generally as DSM III, which considered infantile autism as a subgroup of associated conditions termed 'pervasive developmental disorder'. Following a series of revisions to include the more subtle features of autism, a system for diagnosis was published in DSM IV (1994). This framework forms the basis for diagnosis currently used by many paediatricians.

The other system of classification used by many clinicians is the World Health Organization's 'International Statistical Classification of Diseases and Related Health Problems', or ICD. The edition known as ICD 10 (1993) was the first edition that did not consider autism as a form of psychoses, marking an important point of arrival for the field of autism. ICD 10 (1993) classifies autism as one of several pervasive development conditions ensuring that the basis for diagnosis agreed upon by each of the major systems used by clinicians is developmental.

However, despite the adoption of these systems, the issue of diagnosis remains extremely problematic. This is because autism is defined by what we can see, that is, an individual's behaviour. There is no clear 'marker' which can be clinically obtained and therefore diagnosis reflects the opinion of the diagnostician following observation and interviews with care givers. While for many children, the nature of their condition lends itself easily to diagnosis, there are many children for whom the picture is not clear. This might be for several reasons, including:

1   the manifestation of those features cited as diagnostic criteria in DSM IV and ICD 10 is inconsistent, appearing in certain contexts and apparently not in others

2   the child's condition is complicated by other difficulties such as profound and multiple disabilities, severe learning difficulties, mental health problems or generally poor health

3   the child's developmental history is not fully known, therefore diagnostic tools reliant on developmental checklists are compromised

4   the symptoms of autism may change with age and developmental progress – nevertheless, autism remains a lifelong condition.

In cases such as these the child may remain without a diagnosis for long periods of time. The effect of this can be significantly damaging, with youngsters not able to access appropriate care and education and parents remaining in a diagnostic limbo. However, we must recognise the difficulties faced by diagnosticians, given the broad-ranging spectrum embraced by the condition and the complexity of the individuals within that spectrum.

Prevalence

Recent studies have suggested that early estimates of the prevalence of autism were conservative. Research during the 1990s and into the present century shows significant annual rises in the prevalence of autism with as many as 60 people per 10,000 reported by some researchers (Wing and Potter 2002). The reason for this marked increase is as yet unproven, but may be accounted for by the following factors:

• changes in diagnostic criteria

• the evolution of a concept of a wide spectrum of autistic conditions

• increased awareness and therefore identification of the condition

• possible environmental causes.

Whichever factor, or combination of factors, is in operation, the fact remains that we are finding increasing numbers of children with autism in our schools, an issue which must be urgently addressed. Scott et al. (2002) reported prevalence of 60 per 10,000 of the school population for 5–11-year-olds, while Baird et al. (2006) proposed a figure of 116 per 10,000 of the child population. The National Autistic

Society presents the figure of 1 per cent of the general population and cautions that this may well be a conservative estimate.

Finally, a marked gender bias is consistently reported in studies of prevalence with figures varying from a ratio of 4 males to every 1 female to 8 males to every 1 female. The strong genetic basis for autism bears out these notable gender differences.

Models of autism

Since Kanner's seminal work, there have been a number of models proposed which have sought to explain the prevalent features and characteristics of autism. Each of these models has arisen from a particular paradigm for understanding human psychology and reflects the theoretical background they have emerged from. Consequently, in exploring these models of autism it is important to consider them as providing insights into a particular aspect of autism and not as offering a single global and comprehensive understanding. Our aim should be to try and accommodate these models in a construct of autism which is then applied to the individual and the context we are living or working with. Crucially, we should employ these models to help us understand the experiences of the individual with autism from their perspective, as a tool to support empathy in our practice.

A helpful starting point is Lorna Wing's notion of the **triad of impairments** (Wing and Gould 1979). This model, based on clinical experience and extensive research, recognises core deficits in the areas of

- social interaction

- communication and

- imagination,

and crucially indicates that the severity and manifestation of these fundamental impairments will vary significantly:

> we found that all children with 'autistic features', whether they fitted Kanner's or Asperger's descriptions or had bits and pieces of both, had in common absence or impairments of social interaction, communication and development of imagination. They also had a narrow, rigid, repetitive pattern of activities and interests. The three impairments (referred to as the 'triad') were shown in a wide variety of ways, but the underlying similarities were recognizable. (Wing 1996: 25)

The strength of Wing's model is that it is flexible enough to embrace the full range of the autistic spectrum while remaining conceptually coherent and focused on these three core deficits. A diagrammatic representation of the triad might look something like Figure 1.1, in which the dark grey circle represents impairment in social communication, the pale grey circle impairment in social understanding and the white circle impairment in imagination. Autism occurs where all three circles intersect.

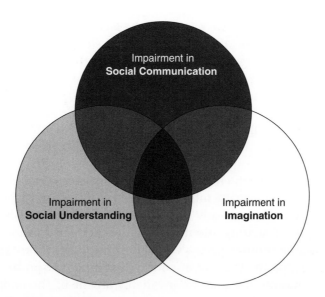

Figure 1.1   The triad of impairment

For educators, in both mainstream and specialist settings, Wing's model allows us to see each child's condition uniquely. While it is necessary for all three impairments to be present, the degree to which each of these components affects the person with autism varies from individual to individual. For some people, one element of the triad may be particularly marked, while others may show significant difficulties across two components and hardly any in the third. For certain people, the overall impact of the triad may be profound, whereas for other people the effects may be comparatively manageable. The infinite possible combinations and permutations of the triad accounts for the huge breadth of the autistic spectrum and the great variety found within it.

A further benefit of this model for educators is that it enables us to reflect on our practice and the environments we practise in from the perspective of a person with impairments in these three crucial areas. Schools are essentially *social* settings which operate through the medium of *communication* and depend upon an *imaginative* negotiation of an infinitely complex and unstable environment. If a person experiences fundamental problems in these key areas, it is little wonder that, regardless of their cognitive potential, schools are difficult places to be.

Another important idea to consider is **mind-blindness** (Baron-Cohen 1990; 1995) which is based on the view that people with autism lack a 'theory of mind'. Simon Baron-Cohen argues that a theory of mind, that is, the ability to appreciate the mental states of oneself and other people, is a prerequisite to effective functioning in social groups. The argument continues that as the human race evolved and societies became increasingly complex and subtle, so the capacity for greater 'social intelligence' increased in order to allow us to process information about the behaviour of others and respond accordingly. This 'adaptive' behaviour is usually evident in children from around the age of 4 onwards. However, children with autism seem to lack the ability to 'think about thoughts' (Happe 1994) suggesting they are impaired in specific but, crucially, not all, areas of socialisation, communication and imagination. As educators we might see the lack of a theory of mind emerging as an inability to grasp the social etiquette of the classroom, an apparent lack of feeling towards peers or a failure to share the excitement that other children may feel. Quite simply, children with autism cannot get inside other people's heads, therefore their understanding of others is profoundly limited.

Early developmental difficulties which may be associated with mind-blindness include problems in infants showing joint attention skills (Sigman et al. 1986), usually evident by 14 months of age and the later failure of children with autism to engage in pretend play (Leslie 1987), which normally emerges between 18 and 24 months old. As a theory of mind is not usually fully developed before 4 years of age, difficulties in these two areas may be seen as early indicators of subsequent problems. In the normally developing child, sharing attention with another person shows an awareness of the separateness of another person's thoughts. Joint attention skills incorporate monitoring or directing the focus of attention of another person through pointing, gestures and gaze monitoring and are invariably absent in the child with autism. Similarly, the ability to engage in pretend play depends upon having a concept of another person's 'mental attitude' (Cohen and Volkmar 1997) towards an object or activity, that is, an awareness that they are pretending too. The failure of this skill to emerge prefigures difficulty in the realm of appreciating other people's thoughts, that is, mind-blindness. For educators, these early signs may be evident in pre-school settings as infants and children appear to be disinterested in activities which captivate other children and fail to engage in the shared fun of pretend play.

The third element which educators need to be aware of relates to the difficulties people with autism have in the area of **executive function**. Executive function is the mechanism which enables us to move our attention flexibly and easily from one activity or object to another. It allows us to plan strategically, solve problems and set ourselves objectives so that we can control our behaviours in planned and meaningful ways (Norman and Shallice 1980). The absence of such a mechanism determines that all our actions are controlled by the environment in response to cues and stimuli, leading to apparently meaningless activity. Without executive function, actions and behaviours compete for dominance in a disorganised and inconsistent manner leading to an inability to plan and execute goal-generated behaviour. In a school setting, this emerges as highly distractible behaviour coupled with a dependence upon ritual and routines and an apparent disregard for the school timetable or the completion of tasks.

A fourth concept which educator's need to consider is that known as **central coherence theory** (Frith 1989). This notion relates to our natural impulse to place information into a context in order to give it meaning. It is usual for human beings to take an overview of things, to look for the 'big picture' and assimilate the detail into that whole. However, people with autism tend to focus on the detail rather than the whole, picking out the minutiae rather than understanding the 'big picture'. It has been found that people with autism show superior abilities in finding the 'embedded figures' from pictures (Shah and Frith 1983) and that children with autism are better able to recognise the identity of familiar faces from a part of the picture than their non-autistic peers (Campbell et al. 1995). Similarly children with autism fail to use context clues when reading (Happe 1994) often mistaking the meaning homophones, for example tear – as in drop – for tear – as in paper. While some of these examples refer to superior ability, this superiority denotes a failure to appreciate the whole and accounts for the piecemeal way in which people with autism acquire knowledge and the unusual cognitive profile presented by many people with autism. Educators may detect the lack of central coherence in the narrowed interests of children with autism, in the ways in which students with autism are often unable to generalise skills or the way in which children with autism often display areas of relative strength described as islets of ability.

A fifth and critical aspect of autism that educators must consider relates to the all pervading impact of **sensory processing** in students with autism. Historically, some degree of sensory difficulty associated with autism had been noted as far back as Kanner's work. However, it is in recent years that difficulty in processing sensory information has gradually come to be recognised by many as a further defining feature of autism. Researchers such as Olga Bogdashina (2003) have focused attention on the sensory-processing difficulties experienced by people with autism, while the work of writers such as Donna Williams (1992) and Wendy Lawson (2000) has provided powerful personal testimony into the impact of these difficulties. More recently, it has been argued that impairments in sensory processing can be regarded as the source of other difficulties commonly associated with autism. Whatever position we might take, sensory-processing difficulties have a profound and pervasive impact on people with autism and must be recognised as such.

Sensory processing difficulties emanate from neurologically based features which determine that people with autism are often either hyper-sensitive or hypo-sensitive to sensory stimuli. Consequently, a person might be extremely sensitive to particular sounds, repulsed by certain smells and tastes, easily distracted by the visual environment or resistant to tactile sensations. Equally, a person might appear not to hear the loudest noises, be prepared to eat or mouth almost anything, apparently not notice the world around them or be able to withstand extremes of temperature or physical pain. Crucially, the same person may have any combination of these features and their presentation may be variable.

Experiencing hyper-sensitive or hypo-sensitive responses to sensory stimuli determines that a person is unable to effectively filter, balance and integrate the sensory input they receive. Consequently, they are bombarded by a cacophony of stimuli which they cannot process effectively into a coherent understanding of their environment. In order to cope with this onslaught of sensory information, people with autism are likely to 'mono-process', that is, focus on one sensory channel. This results in the person being unable to process more than one element of sensory input at a time. Therefore, the person may not be able to look at someone else while they are listening to them or sit still while they are looking at something.

The implications of this for the person with autism are profound and far-reaching. Forming relationships, remaining safe in a chaotic environment and learning in the rich and varied stimulus of the modern classroom are all severely compromised by the inability to process sensory input effectively and consistently. It is little wonder that this feature of autism has assumed such importance over the last few years.

The concepts described above represent part of the conceptual framework which underpins current thinking in the field of autism. It is important to consider this framework as developing dynamically as our knowledge of the condition increases. However, the ideas discussed above are well founded and remain established as significant agents in our understanding of autism and are of particular use to the educator engaged in identifying those features of the learner which represent relative strengths and those which present the learner with challenges. Whatever way we choose to view the learner with autism, we must adopt a holistic view which incorporates those qualities that support their progress, those elements of the condition that can be a barrier to their learning and, crucially, the person in and among the conceptual framework.

A changing context

The field of autism is currently among the most active domains in terms of research and the development of ideas and practice across the world. Geneticists, psychologists, neurologists, educators, legislators and social care commissioners and providers are making significant progress towards improving outcomes for people with autism, and people with autism are consistently proving themselves to be valuable and valued members of society.

In England, the Autism Act came into force in November 2009 and became the first piece of UK legislation focused on a specific condition. This Act placed a duty on the government to produce an autism strategy for adults by April 2010 and to issue statutory guidance to local authorities and local health bodies in respect of supporting the needs of adults with autism by the end of 2010. It is important to recognise that there is a long journey from legislation to an improved quality of life; nonetheless, it is encouraging to consider that the young people educators are working with today will experience better opportunities as adults than those of previous generations.

Legislative bodies in other areas of the UK have addressed the development of a national approach to autism. As far back as 2002 the Welsh Assembly was working on a strategic plan for autism while, more recently, the Scottish government produced a draft Scottish Autism Strategy. This governmental intent across the UK indicates that there is a clear recognition of the need to address the needs of people with autism in a strategic and coherent manner.

Alongside these legislative changes, there are distinct societal changes that will hopefully lead to a better quality of life for people with autism. Increased coverage in the media has led to a greater public awareness of the condition and although some of that coverage may be lurid or sentimental most of it serves some purpose in promoting an understanding of autism. As public awareness grows it is likely that acceptance of the condition and its associated strengths will grow proportionately.

Of course it is not only the media that can support this process of increasing awareness. Organisations such as the National Autistic Society, the Scottish Society for Autism, Autism Cymru, the Autism Education Trust and a plethora of regional and local autism societies are unstinting in their promotion of the understanding of autism and provide support networks for parents and professionals alike.

This increasing social awareness is coupled with significant breakthroughs in the fields of scientific and medical research. The Autism Genome Project is a large scale international collaboration which is endeavouring to identify the genetic architecture of autism. The AGP has published over 200 papers on autism since 2003 with scientists from over 50 research centres working together. Phase One of the project which ran from 2004–2007 established the world's largest gene bank for autism, providing the most comprehensive database of autism available. This Phase of the project also produced the most comprehensive genome scan into the genetics of autism.

Phase Two of the AGP was launched in 2007 and focused on identifying meaningful genetic variants associated with autism. The final set of reports from Phase Two began emerging in the Summer of 2010 and papers relating to this period of research are continuing to be published as the AGP endeavours to secure funding for a Third phase of research.

The momentum behind research into the genetic nature of autism is replicated in other medical and scientific fields as researchers seek to identify causative factors and interventions which might ameliorate the condition. Recently, the Medical Research Council reported a pioneering approach to diagnosis in adults using brain scan technology, while a burgeoning body of research is focused on developing nutritional interventions for people with autism (MRC Press release 10 August 2010 and www.mrc.ac.uk/Newspublications/News/MRC007083).

Autism remains an enigmatic condition deeply rooted in the most complex of aspects of humanity. However, the context around autism is rapidly evolving as new learning gathers speed, propelling our understanding of autism forward in what is potentially an exciting and beneficial future.

Key points for reflection

- In what ways has our understanding of autism developed since Kanner's original work in 1943?
- Visit the Autism Genome Project's website in order to keep up to date with important discoveries in this area.
- Think about a child or young person with autism who you know. Try and integrate the various models of autism described in this chapter to develop a holistic understanding of that person.

Further reading

1 Bogdashina, O. (2003) *Sensory Perceptual Issues in Autism and Asperger Syndrome: Different Sensory Experiences, Different Perceptual Worlds.* London and Philadelphia, PA: Jessica Kingsley. A critical text in supporting our understanding of the profound and lifelong effect of sensory processing difficulties; provides the very useful Sensory Profile Checklist – Revised (SPCR).

2 Lawson, W. (2000) *Life Behind Glass: A Personal Account of Autism Spectrum Disorder.* London and Philadelphia, PA: Jessica Kingsley. A beautifully written account from the frontline, describing the experiences of the individual with autism from their perspective as a 'permanent onlooker'.

3   Williams, D. (1992) *Nobody Nowhere*. London and Philadelphia, PA: Jessica Kingsley. A moving personal narrative focusing on the isolation experienced by the writer in a strange and confusing world.

4   Wing, L. (1996) *The Autistic Spectrum*. London: Constable and Robinson. A seminal text which stands the test of time and is a must for anyone starting out in the field.

Useful links

1   www.aspiedebi.com

2   www.autism.org.uk

3   www.autismgenome.org

4   www.autismeducationtrust.org.uk

2

The impact of autism on learning

> **This chapter:**
>
> - **Presents the impact of autism on learning as consisting of three waves affecting the whole child**
> - **Discusses how this impact affects the individual, their learning, their family, professionals and peers**

As practitioners working with children and young people with autism, we must ask ourselves how that element of 'who they are' will affect the way in which they learn. The quality of our practice depends on how we move from *knowing* about the condition towards *understanding* how autism affects the individual's learning style, what strengths it brings and what barriers to learning it may cause. This ability to think beyond the textbook, to integrate knowledge, understanding and empathy, is vital because there is no such thing as a 'textbook' child with autism. While every child is unique, children with autism have a unique uniqueness. Consequently, we cannot follow a prescribed, 'one-size-fits-all' formula but need to develop approaches which address the needs of each individual.

Autism can be seen as having three 'waves' of impact on the child's learning which radiate outwards from the child. These three waves are:

1. the **effect** of the condition itself

2. **behaviour** which occurs as a result of the condition

3. **attitudes** which form as a consequence of the child's behaviour.

The first of these incorporates those primary features of autism which directly affect the child's learning, such as, communication difficulties, rigidity, sensory issues or problems with organising their thoughts. These, in turn, cause a second wave of impact which is characterised by the behavioural features associated with autism. These behavioural issues trigger a third wave of impact which is defined by the relationships and attitudes the child forms with the world around them. This model is illustrated in Figure 2.1.

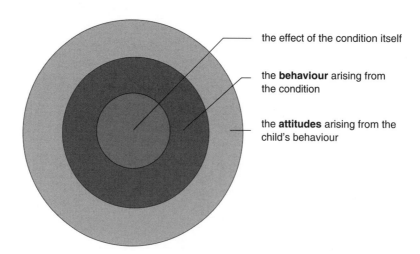

the effect of the condition itself

the **behaviour** arising from the condition

the **attitudes** arising from the child's behaviour

Figure 2.1   Autism: three waves of impact

The effect of the condition

This level of impact is an immediate consequence of the child's autism. Although the impact of the condition is inevitable, it can be obscured by other factors that accumulate around the child. For the practitioner to make a positive contribution to the learning of the child with autism, it is necessary to develop an understanding of the child which is rooted in the nature of the condition. This is achieved not only through increasing our knowledge but also by evolving a 'perceptive sympathy' which enables the practitioner to see through to the child and the impact of autism on the child's learning.

Social impairment in the classroom

Walk into any classroom, in any school, and what immediately strikes you? Essentially, that you have entered an infinitely complex and sophisticated social environment. Most of us have found classroom society difficult to cope with at some point, and this should be no surprise. Classrooms can be confusing places with subtle and inconsistent social rules, shifting allegiances and power constantly changing hands. As an antidote to this, we adopt a role within the culture of the classroom, whether it be the joker, the chameleon, the sporting hero, the swot, the social butterfly or the bully. We all look to perform some function in the social mechanism because we have an innate understanding of the social role expected of us and that we expect of others.

However, if you have autism, how do you negotiate this daunting passage of your life. It is difficult enough for those without an autistic spectrum condition (ASC) so how much harder must it be for the child whose innate understanding of society is impaired; for the child who does not see what everybody else sees or think the way that everybody else thinks. Consider the fundamental obstacles to a child's social functioning brought about by impairments in the ability to:

- read social situations

- understand social codes and expectations

- interpret facial expression and body language

- appreciate other people's feelings

- engage other people through social 'devices' (smiles and small talk)

- determine the important components of social interaction

- organise actions into orthodox patterns.

It is arguable that for almost any other special need, the classroom only becomes disabling when a demand to perform a given task is made. For the child with autism, the classroom itself is disabling. For many children with autism, disability begins at the door.

Communication difficulties

Another inescapable feature of any classroom is that it is a communication-dense environment. The classroom, is alive with a myriad of communicative acts, some hidden, some obvious, some deliberate, many unintentional. This pertains to all classrooms, in mainstream, special or specialist schools; indeed it applies to all environments in which children learn.

So, for the child whose communication skills are impaired, this rich, fast-flowing stream of communication may seem more like a tidal wave of 'sound and fury, signifying nothing' Shakespeare's *Macbeth*, 5:5. Consider the difficulties in effectively engaging in the communicative environment of a classroom from the perspective of a child who is unable to:

- comprehend much of what is said to him

- adequately express his thoughts, needs, emotions, wishes

- discriminate which language is intended for him

- discern a person's tone of voice and what it might mean

- understand humour, idiom, sarcasm

- initiate communication

- recognise the need to reciprocate communication.

Impairments in communication place the child with autism in an alien world which is confusing, frightening and unintelligible. The spoken word flies past, peppered with sudden unexplained outbursts. Non-verbal communication is a cacophony of frowns, furrows and jerks which is meaningless and often threatening.

Inflexible thinking in a dynamic environment

When children play, they exercise that most important of human faculties – the ability to think adaptively. They become increasingly skilled in the exploration of their thoughts and soon are tasting tea in empty plastic cups, hearing teddy read and seeing elephants in banks of clouds. And while all of this is lovely to watch and join in with, it serves an evolutionary purpose. From these playful groundings, human beings learn to adapt to the chaotic, to formulate flexible structures which organise their lives and yet allow for the quakes and shakes of the real world.

In many ways schools are working examples of evolutionary processes, of adaptation to the environment, of survival. From the earliest years in nurseries, children are required to think with a sophistication that seems beyond their years. In any classroom, in any school, we will encounter a number of situations which demand that the child thinks imaginatively, flexibly and adaptively. Children gather on the floor for story-time, drive diggers through the sand, write as if they are Victorian child labourers, design maps of non-existent cities, carry messages to teachers they have never met, choose subjects to suit careers they have not yet embarked on. All of this requires a fantastic imaginative effort. Not to mention the disputes and difficulties, the taking of turns, the avoiding of trouble and the very necessary day-dreaming. Again all dependent on imagination, all necessitating flexible thinking and adaptive behaviour.

But, if your autism disables you in the social slalom of the classroom, it is likely that you will either rush headlong downhill unable to deviate from your course or, perhaps, not even start the race, opting out entirely. Consider the 'unseen world' of the classroom from the point of view of the child who is unable to:

- engage in pretend play

- project themselves into future situations

- comprehend a world outside their experiences

- access elements of the curriculum which rely on imagination

- understand deception

- think how others might think or feel.

The difficulties caused by impairment in the realm of imagination are significant and far-reaching. If we consider play as the foundation of learning, then impairment in a child's ability to engage meaningfully in play, presents fundamental obstacles to that child.

Sensory processing in a sensational world

Our earliest experiences are mediated through our senses. Our senses help us to make sense of the world around us, to navigate our environments and to determine our likes, dislikes, fears and passions. At a fundamental level, we are shaped by our senses as they formulate our understanding and lay the pathways for our learning. Sensory experiences are brought to us through seven key channels which are:

1 visual – what we see

2 auditory – what we hear

3 olfactory – what we smell

4 gustatory – what we taste

5 tactile – what we feel

6 vestibular – where we are in relation to the world or balance

7 proprioceptory – where we are in relation to ourselves or co-ordination.

These seven channels work in a co-ordinated and integrated way to apprehend the world around us and assimilate the information we obtain into a coherent understanding. From this foundation we develop into the people we become and continue to be.

By their very nature, schools are sensational places. Educators understand how children learn through their senses and actively promote stimulating and exciting environments in order to promote learning. We purposefully create beautiful visual displays, play lively music or engage students in energetic physical activities. We deliberately encourage children to play in sand, balance on a beam or try new tastes and smells. All of this is deeply beneficial to the child who is able to process the incoming sensory information effectively.

Alongside this purposefully contrived sensory environment, the school is a jungle of sensory experiences. Playgrounds are a cacophony of shouts, screams, laughter and tears while corridors heave and rush with the comings and goings of hundreds of people. Dining halls clang and clatter and smell different every day. In classrooms noises change all the time, sometimes quiet, sometimes loud, sometimes people talking, sometimes computer fans whirring. All of this is neatly assimilated by the child who is able to integrate these sensations with their previous knowledge.

However, if a child experiences difficulties in processing sensory information, this sensational environment can be a very frightening place which at best is not conducive to learning and at worst creates phobia. Therefore for the learner with autism, we need to be considering the profound impact difficulties with sensory processing will have particularly when we consider how many people with autism regard their condition as essentially relating to sensory processing.

As ever, in the world of autism nothing is straightforward. Sensory-processing difficulties seem to exist on a continuum ranging from slight inconsistencies at one end to a wholly fragmented perception of the environment at another. To complicate this further an individual may experience a severe difficulty in one of the seven senses and no significant impairment among any of the others. Equally, difficulties may appear in any combinations and degrees across all seven areas providing an almost infinite array of presentations. To compound this, difficulties may vary in an individual from day to day in relation to any number of factors such as health, emotional state or time of the year.

While sensory processing difficulties emerge from an extremely complex series of neurological mechanisms, in simple terms, people with autism either experience *hyper-sensitivity* or *hypo-sensitivity* to sensory stimuli. This means that they experience sensory input differently to people who are 'neuro-typical'. If a person is hyper-sensitive to a particular stimuli, they experience it more powerfully than other people; if a person is hypo-sensitive to a stimuli they experience it less powerfully than other people.

These extremes of experience affect a person's ability to manage incoming sensory information so that sights, sounds, smells and all manner of sensations are scrambled into an incoherent stream of stimuli. This determines that the individual is unlikely to be able to distinguish between foreground and background information creating what has become known as a 'Gestalt perception'. Consequently, the individual does not easily discriminate between relevant and irrelevant information in a given context. Arguably, relevance is a subjective term based on social norms but in a classroom scenario not being able to distinguish between the teacher's voice and the tick of a clock can be extremely disabling.

One way in which it is thought that people with autism cope with this sensory overload is by tuning into one modality, a phenomenon known as *mono-processing*. While neuro-typical people ordinarily operate all of their senses simultaneously, people with autism appear to focus on one single sensory channel. Therefore, if an individual has tuned into the visual channel they may be able to detect every minute detail of an object but not hear anything or smell anything while they are fixed into this modality. It is important to remember that there will be degrees and varieties of mono-processing, but in some form, this coping mechanism will be evident.

Any place of learning, be it a nursery, school, college or university is awash with sensory stimuli which are both intentional and incidental. People engaged in these places are required to assimilate these stimuli and make sense of their sensations. Consider the learning environment from the perspective of an individual who experiences sensory processing difficulties and is therefore limited in their capacity to:

- filter incoming sensory information

- identify relevant stimuli

- tolerate everyday sensations

- perceive potentially harmful experiences

- absorb information via several channels simultaneously

- move from one sensory input to another.

Difficulties in the arena of sensory processing fundamentally inhibit a person's ability to navigate their way around their environment. Where the sensory impairment is obvious, for example if a person is visually impaired or hearing impaired, it is possible to easily identify this and compensate accordingly. Where the sensory impairment is hidden because it lies within the processing mechanisms of the brain, it is less easy to identify and even more difficult to compensate for. As is often the case in autism, it is the covert nature of the condition which is most disabling.

Behavioural issues: fear, flight and fight

Autism is a 'behaviourally defined condition' (Charman and Care 2004). There is no chromosomal marker, no physiological feature which tells us a child has autism. It is only by observing the child's behaviour that we can say that the child has an ASC and only by analysing that behaviour further that we can develop strategies to meet the child's needs.

Fear

For children with autism, fear can be a dominant and often overpowering state of being. This can be seen as a direct consequence of severe difficulties in interpreting the world around them, in understanding what is happening to them or is going to happen to them. Naturally, if your ability to learn is restricted by the primary impact of the condition you experience, then more things remain unknown to you and, consequently, there are more things to be afraid of. Whereas for most children encouragement from adults or peer pressure leads them to experience new things, for the child with autism the value of adult praise or the shame of losing face means very little. There is, therefore, little incentive to step into new territory.

Equally, if you perceive things in different ways to others, either because of sensory problems or because of the way your brain processes information, then you may well learn to be afraid of many things that other people are not fearful of, while remaining unafraid of many things which are a danger to you. This may manifest itself as the child who sees no peril in darting across the busy dual carriageway and yet finds walking down the school corridor absolutely petrifying. Furthermore, fear breeds fear, so that associated objects become objects of fear themselves. The child who is scared of the supermarket because it is packed with strange people, noises and smells, develops a fear of the coat he is putting on to go to the supermarket because he comes to learn what putting that coat on might mean. Subsequently, he develops a fear of coats of any type and refuses in the depths of winter to wear anything more than a T-shirt.

The consequence of such fear is that in addition to the difficulties the child faces due to autism, there is a layer of fear and tension which can suffocate their learning and enjoyment of life. This capsule of fear is both important and necessary to the child, and any attempts to draw the child from it must be considered and gradual. However, in order to enable features of the primary impact to be adequately addressed, it is vital that this layer of fear is gradually dissolved.

Flight

Flight enables us to escape danger. In everyday life it helps us avoid uncomfortable situations with a range of subtle and sophisticated strategies. For the child with autism, flight is often an effective and well-practised defence mechanism. However, as a pattern of behaviour, flight is invariably incompatible with the context the child is operating in. Within the classroom flight can manifest in several distinct ways, namely:

1   running away

2   refusal

3   self-absorption

4   obsession.

These behaviours may occur alone, in combinations simultaneously or in a sequence, often a predictable series. Given the breadth of the autistic spectrum and the broad range of backgrounds and personalities involved, we may encounter a child whose initial response to demands is to run out of the classroom or dive under the nearest table. We might know of children who skilfully turn every topic of conversation towards their own particular interests or children who are apparently locked into flickering their fingers centimetres from their eyes. Though varied, each of these is a form of escape, a way of displacing the discomfort of the here and now with a form of behaviour which the child is master of and the outcome of which is within the child's control.

As practitioners we must recognise that the flight behaviour is functionally significant for the child and our approaches towards reducing the behaviour must be informed by the child's need to escape situations they find difficult. However, as with addressing a child's fear, it is only when we can engage the child that we can positively affect their learning.

Fight

While by no means a necessary consequence of autism, there are associations between autism and aggressive behaviour which is the result of the frustrations and fears people with autism experience as a consequence of their condition. It is usually the fight response which has the most immediate effect on the context the child with autism is in and is consequently the response which is most hastily addressed. This is unfortunate given the fact that, invariably, the need to fight emerges if other levels of need have not been adequately understood and addressed. Consequently, we deal with the crisis rather than those factors which lead to the crisis.

For the child with autism whose needs are not adequately addressed, fighting becomes an effective and rapid means of getting those needs addressed. For those people with autism who experience significant learning difficulties, the capacity to develop other, more appropriate strategies for meeting those needs is very limited. Consequently, the child becomes increasingly dependent upon fighting in order to meet their needs and narrows the already limited range of strategies further in an ever decreasing spiral.

For some people with autism, this decline into aggressive and damaging behaviour has resulted in tragically restricted and oppressed lives, foreshortened by the consequences of their behaviour such as self-injurious behaviour, physical trauma or medical intervention.

Attitudes to autism

This level of impact occurs as a result of the interaction between people with autism and others. It is the area of impact which we can most readily affect by increasing our own personal knowledge of the condition and sharing this with colleagues across all sectors.

Parents

Working closely with parents and families is essential for effective practice in the field of autism. Children with autism are complex and enigmatic (Frith 1989), and no single person can be expected to design and implement a uniformly effective learning programme for such children. Consequently, liaison with parents is of paramount importance at every stage of the child's progress. Practitioners need to be guided by policies based upon well-founded practice and supported by senior managers whose organisations are open and honest.

Working with parents requires practitioners to be aware of the 'journey' parents may well have endured before the relationship is established. Depending upon the age of the child and the severity of the condition, parents may be experiencing a range of different emotions, including:

1 **grief** – parents whose child has been recently diagnosed with autism are often at an early stage of adjusting to the news. This adjustment includes an indefinite period of grief during which parents may suffer from denial of the condition, depression or guilt

2 **anger** – this may be directed at services which they feel have failed their child or the attitudes of other people towards their child

3 **anxiety** – this can be focused on issues in the past, the present or the future and may involve concerns not only about the child with autism but also regarding siblings, partners and other family members

A person's response to these emotions will vary significantly and produce a range of attitudes, including:

1 **cynicism** – parents whose experiences are dominated by a failure of services to support their child and family will naturally doubt that any professional is able or willing to provide that support

2 **optimism** – for some people, the start of their relationship with a dedicated practitioner will be seen as a new opportunity to improve matters for their child and family. They will draw on the knowledge of previous failures to shape a positive future for their child

3 **defensiveness** – collaboration with parents always carries a danger of intrusion and it is wise to exercise caution and invite collaboration rather than foist it upon people. Many parents may be distrustful of professionals who might be perceived as wanting to run their lives

4 **openness** – where an atmosphere of trust and mutual respect has been nurtured, parents are able to share information about their child, enabling a whole picture of the child to emerge

5 **isolationist** – many parents describe their child's condition as disabling the whole family. Some parents report that their social life and their relationships with their extended family are severely affected and that they feel isolated and alone. This in turn can lead to distrust and extremely low self-esteem resulting in parents attempting to 'go it alone' as they perceive support will not be forthcoming

6 **collaborative** – if individuals have access to networks of other parents of children with autism then it is possible to forge positive and fruitful relationships within these groups. People understand one another's difficulties and work together towards a common purpose.

Each of these attitudinal states can be seen to describe polar opposites. Commonly it is a combination of a person's character, their experiences of services and the quality of support around them that shapes their attitudes. As practitioners we usually inherit people's attitudes. Our aim should be to foster attitudes which are at the positive end of the continuum.

Peers

As experienced practitioners in the field of ASC we often struggle to understand the way in which students with autism act or are uncomfortable with the behaviour some students with autism display. It is not surprising, therefore, that many of their peers will be confused or disturbed by the actions and patterns of behaviour of their classmate with autism.

For some children this lack of understanding may result in a refreshing acceptance of the child with autism for the person they are. However, some children may be fearful and this may result in ostracising, bullying or mocking the child with autism. These attitudes create a matrix of difficulties for the child with ASC which exacerbate their already significant impairments in forming peer relationships. For example, a child who has problems with initiating social contact, may find that on attempting to interact with his peers, his endeavours are rejected, perhaps quite cruelly. Consequently, the incentive to attempt further interactions diminishes, reducing the opportunities for the child to practice and develop his skills, thereby establishing a vicious, ever decreasing, circle of isolation.

For many children with autism, the older they become the wider the gap between them and their peers grows. This is due in part to the increasing pressures of conformity which their peers experience as they approach adulthood and the need the majority of us have to belong to the group. Children with autism tend not to care for groups and are therefore excluded from the smaller units of friendship which might be appropriate to their needs.

Professionals

In many ways, a positive attitude towards students with autism is directly related to a person's understanding of the condition. Working with youngsters with ASC is very enjoyable and fulfilling and yet there is much about the condition which professionals can find de-skilling. For example, children with autism can be reserved, aloof, seemingly uninterested and dismissive of our best efforts. They can appear not to care about their peers or about their relationship with us as educators. This goes to the heart of what we do; as educationalists we pride ourselves on the ability to stimulate, to inspire, to build enduring relationships with children. If this is rejected, we are left with nothing to define us. It is, perhaps, a form of defence that can cause some professionals to see the child with ASC as rude, unmanageable and beyond the scope of their talents.

A result of this is that some professionals are wary of working with children with ASC. Often this is rationalised as seeing the child as detrimental to the greater good of the school or class or presented as the school being unable to meet the child's needs given the environmental restrictions. Such standpoints may have validity in certain contexts. However, the increasing prevalence of the condition and the momentum behind the inclusion agenda challenges these standpoints and is driving change in these contexts.

Professionals must be supported in developing their knowledge and understanding of autism in order to enable them to address the needs of students with ASC. While the pressures to achieve this are significant, there are increasing opportunities for professionals to develop their understanding and knowledge of the condition and a variety of ways in which this might be achieved. The materials produced for the 2009 Inclusion Development Programme (IDP) focused on autism provide a solid foundation for developing understanding, while a range of organisations offer further training in order to enhance and refine that understanding. Further details of these are provided in Chapter 3.

> ### ⚡ Key points for reflection
>
> - Which of the three waves of impact do you feel best equipped to address? Why is this?
> - Have you explored the 2009 Inclusion Development Project materials focused on autism? Could these support your practice?
> - Think about the context in which you live or work. How might the sensory environment be affecting the child or young person with autism? What beneficial changes could you bring about?

Further reading

1 Atwood, T. (1998) *Asperger's Syndrome: A Guide for Parents and Professionals.* London and Philadelphia, PA: Jessica Kingsley. If you only read one text on Asperger's syndrome, make sure it is this enduring and accessible guide.

2   Jordan, R. and Powell, S. (1995) *Understanding and Teaching Children with Autism.* Chichester: John Wiley. This book explores the learning of children with autism from the perspective of the child and offers practical yet theory rich support for the practitioner.

3   Howlin, P., Baron-Cohen, S. and Hadwin, J. (1999) *Teaching Children With Autism to Mind-Read: A Practical Guide.* Chichester: John Wiley. This work addresses the infinitely complex domain of human thinking in a straightforward and helpful way.

4   Moyes, R.A. (2001) *Incorporating Social Goals in the Classroom: A Guide for Teachers and Parents of Children with High-Functioning Autism and Asperger's Syndrome.* London and Philadelphia, PA: Jessica Kingsley. Focused on the more able population, this book offers insights into the ways in which we can support social skills among these children and young people.

Useful links

1   www.jkp.com/mindreading/specialneeds/

2   http://nationalstrategies.standards.dcsf.gov.uk/node/289529

3   http://nationalstrategies.standards.dcsf.gov.uk/node/165037

3

Sharing positive attitudes towards students with autism

This chapter:

- **Suggests ways in which positive attitudes towards students with autism can be promoted by increasing people's understanding of the condition**
- **Provides strategies to support practitioners in sharing knowledge with colleagues including INSET materials**

Part of our work as practitioners involved with students with autistic spectrum conditions is to promote and sustain positive attitudes towards children and young people with autism. We can achieve this by addressing the third level of impact on the child's learning, namely, people's attitudes. This level of impact presents us with opportunities for immediate gains. In this area we are largely dealing with issues of sharing knowledge and understanding, in winning hearts and minds. This is undoubtedly a challenging objective which should not be underestimated. However, it is an accessible challenge in which the key factors are related to time and resources, as oppose to those 'within child' factors which will be encountered at the other levels of impact.

Working with professionals

A professional's attitude towards students with ASC is directly related to their knowledge and understanding of the condition. Consequently, there is a need to develop systems and means by which knowledge and understanding are shared with colleagues. Understandably, we are in competition with a multitude of other demands on practitioners and therefore need to promote information in an accessible and manageable form which is tailored to the context the person is working in. The depth of knowledge required by a person might lie on a continuum from 'awareness' to 'expertise' determined by the role they perform. Colleagues whose only contact with students with autism is during break-times or assemblies will need a different level of understanding to those colleagues who may share the same teaching space. Similarly these colleagues' needs will differ again from those people primarily responsible for the teaching of youngsters with an ASC.

Responding to this continuum of professional development need, our training 'portfolio' might include

- informal approaches

- INSET days

- outreach

- accredited courses

- resources,

each of which depends upon practitioners within the field promoting the cause of students with ASC in a positive and proactive manner. Of the many myths which surround autism, the belief that working effectively with students with an ASC is only open to a minority of highly specialised experts, is among the least helpful. As practitioners in the field, we must show colleagues that our practice is attainable to anyone who is committed to good practice and is willing to learn. Essentially, we must show other practitioners that, like themselves, we are working with children, children that need specific approaches, but still children.

Informal approaches

Some of the most effective professional development takes place over cups of coffee. Share your work with your colleagues in the staffroom, over lunch on training days or at staff meetings and briefings. Above all, share your enthusiasm, present your work as attainable and your students as accessible.

 Suggestion box

Encourage colleagues to visit your classroom or school in order to observe your practice. Ensure that you have planned adequate time for discussion after the observations. Base your discussions on the **impact** autism has on the child, the **strategies** you use to address this and the **progress** the child is making as a result of this. You might structure their observations by giving them a checklist of issues to consider (see figure 3.1) while they are observing. Invite colleagues into your workplace before they have a 'crisis'. Increase their knowledge before major difficulties arise.

N.B. It is in the nature of practitioners to want to get involved in the activity, to be hands on. However, in the field of autism, observation is a crucial component of practice. Insist that any professional visitor simply sits still and watches for a significant proportion of the time they spend with you. If necessary, velcro them to the chair!

1. What do you notice about the child's learning environment?

2. Does the pace of work differ from that of your practice?

3. How is language used?

4. What strategies are used to support understanding?

5. How would you characterise the interactions between child and adult?

6. What barriers to learning do you think the child may be experiencing?

7. How might you adapt your practice to meet this child's needs?

8. How engaged in the adult directed activities is the child?

9. How does the child indicate his/her needs?

10. What does the child seem to find rewarding?

Figure 3.1   Observation checklist

Photocopiable:
Educating Students on the Autistic Spectrum © Martin Hanbury, 2012 (SAGE)

Please photocopy this checklist, adapting it as necessary to the context you are working in and the nature of your relationship with the person observing.

INSET days

The competition for INSET space is fierce and growing fiercer with each new Government initiative. Training for colleagues must be accessible and context driven. At this level of input, most people will want to know how to address issues in their own practice rather than become expert in the field. There are materials for INSET available in the appendix of this book which can be adapted to the context, enabling practitioners to reflect on their current practice and identify ways in which to move practice forward.

Outreach

Outreach takes many forms and is different things to different people in differing contexts. However, a general view would be that it involves supporting a child by sharing specific skills and knowledge, germane to the needs of the child. Successful outreach is characterised by the seven Cs, namely:

1 Clarity

2 Consensus

3 Contract

4 Child-centred

5 Credible Practitioners

6 Consistency

7 Collaboration.

This can be expressed as **clear** agreements between all parties involved in the project, arrived at via **consensus**, defined by a 'contract' and focused entirely on the needs of the **child**. Outreach must be delivered by **credible** 'specialists' supporting the work of organisations with **consistency** in terms of knowledge shared, persons involved and the regularity of contact. Effective outreach is essentially **collaborative**, involving committed practitioners sharing expertise rather than one party 'doing' outreach to another.

Continuing professional development

As previously indicated the 2009 Inclusion Development Programme materials provide a useful foundation for professional development. These can be accessed at:

http://nationalstrategies.standards.dcsf.gov.uk/node/289529 for students in the Early Years and

http://nationalstrategies.standards.dcsf.gov.uk/node/165037 for Primary and Secondary Phase students.

In order to develop knowledge and understanding further professionals can access a broad variety of courses many of which are taught in a modular form and increasing numbers of which are web based. The National Autistic Society provide a detailed list of available courses at:

http://www.autism.org.uk/working-with/services-for-professionals/courses-for-professionals-in-autism-and-other-related-topics.aspx

Resources

Always at a premium, appropriate resources are essential for people looking to work effectively with youngsters with ASC. Resources may include a well-developed library relating to issues in autism, software and facilities for producing bespoke materials for students, communication aids, cause-and-effect toys and particular areas of your classroom or school such as a soft-play area or multi-sensory room. Sharing resources with colleagues enables them to trial items with children without having to waste money. Another noticeable phenomenon is the way in which people tend to listen much more attentively when resources are on offer!

Nurturing home–school relationships

For any child, the quality of the relationship between home and school has a profound effect on their learning. For a child with autism, this relationship is especially important in order to ensure effective communication and enable consistency across settings. Positive relationships between parents and practitioners are characterised by the following key elements:

- approachable practitioners

- openness, honesty and trust

- sharing ideas

- records of contact,

each of which must be continuously monitored and explicitly valued.

Approachable practitioners

First impressions count for a lot! If parents are put off by their initial contact with practitioners or organisations, it is hard to regain the trust and respect which are the lifeblood of any successful relationship. Approachability depends to some extent on a person's nature; however, there are strategies which can be adopted to ensure that an individual or organisation is as approachable as possible.

Suggestion box

- Make a concerted effort to welcome parents into your school or classroom. Structure this so that learning is not disrupted.

- Make a point of contacting parents to give good news of their child's achievements; celebrate their successes. Avoid only ever speaking to parents about problems.

- Offer to visit the child's home. Seeing the home context will increase your understanding of the whole child. Be aware that some parents may find this intrusive and in some circumstances it might be prudent to visit with another colleague.

- Try and establish a space within your school which the parents can consider their own. Create a learning resource within this space, a parent library and information point.

- Parent workshops focused on issues related to autism can be supportive and encourage parents into the school.

Openness, honesty and trust

These three elements are inextricably linked and mutually reliant. The last of these, trust, is the ultimate aim but is not attainable without the first two components. Trust can be hard to win if parents' previous experiences with professionals have been negative. It is doubly important in such cases to be explicitly open and consistently honest. At times there will be the need to discuss difficult and sensitive issues; avoiding such issues will damage your relationship with parents, while inept handling of the situation will ruin the relationship completely. Take time to plan carefully what you will say and how you will say it. Record everything that is discussed and share these minutes with parents. Where necessary include other colleagues in order to support your interpretation of the issues that are discussed.

Sharing ideas

As practitioners we have much to learn about the children we work with. They are typically complex and present unique characteristics which challenge our understanding and patterns of practice. We may hope to develop expertise, yet it is the child's parents who are the experts, that is, experts with regard to their child. The opportunity to share ideas allows us to combine expertise with experts' views. Such opportunities may vary in scale from informal discussions between one parent and one practitioner, to conferences involving many interested parties. Whichever medium is chosen to share ideas, it is crucial to engender an ethos in which every person feels their ideas have value, that their perspectives have importance. Depending on the context you are working in, you may need to state this explicitly in order to encourage people who may be intimidated by professionals or suffering from low self-confidence due to the difficulties they are encountering with their child.

Suggestion box

Offer a programme of parent workshops for your parent group. In a mainstream setting, you may only have one or two families for whom these workshops are relevant. In this case, try and combine with neigbouring schools to form a cluster focusing on issues in autism.

In the first instance, invite parents to a coffee morning and, during this, ask parents to identify issues which they would like to focus on. Devise a series of regular meetings addressing each issue in turn. Try and deliver the workshops in a variety of ways in order to suit both the content of the workshop and the range of learning styles within the parent group. Engage outside speakers for some of the workshops in order to widen perspectives.

Records of contact

We live in an 'evidence-based' age, a time when we are required to record almost every professional action or decision process. Maintaining and sharing records of contact with parents provides a basis for mutual understanding as all parties have a common record to refer to when seeking clarification or planning ahead. A well-maintained, well-written home–school diary can act as a voice for the child with autism and an invaluable source of ideas and suggestions between parents and practitioners. A log book of significant telephone conversations between parents and practitioners provides a record of issues which have been discussed offering support where necessary.

Peer relationships

Sharing a class with a child with autism cannot be easy; even, perhaps especially, if you are a child with autism yourself. Consequently, we should be looking for as many ways as possible to equip children who are in the same class as students with autism, with the skills which will enable them to cope with this demanding situation.

The development of these necessary skills is based on an expanding understanding of autism among students, centred around:

- increasing awareness of the condition

- developing understanding of individual's needs

- recognising achievement

- deflating peer pressure.

Progress in any one of these areas leads to progress in one of the others; progress in all, leads to an increased understanding among all students.

Before embarking upon any form of information sharing with students it is crucial to determine the extent to which the child with autism is aware of their condition and the degree to which they might want that knowledge shared. This is an ethical minefield which can only be successfully negotiated through extensive consultation with the student, the child's family, colleagues and organisations dedicated to the field of autism. In certain circumstances it may be necessary to postpone initiatives to share knowledge about autism; the best interests of the child with autism must determine this decision.

Increasing awareness

A continuous programme of information about autism will increase the knowledge and understanding of the condition among the child's peers. The nature of this programme will vary according to the learning ability and maturity of the students in the class. However, certain features will be universal. For example, there will be the need to introduce the concepts – if not the terminology – of those components of the condition which account for much of the behaviour that will be observed. Similarly, children may benefit from learning about the prevalence of autism in their community in order to prepare them for future contact with people with an ASC.

 ### Suggestion box

For younger children, diagrams can be used to present the triad of impairment as a strong but simple model. Younger students will benefit by hands on experience of Picture Exchange Communication System (PECS) books and Treatment and Education of Autistic and related Communication handicapped Children (TEACCH) schedules and the use of video to observe how people with autism use these resources.

For older, able students, the shared reading of texts such as Mark Haddon's (2003) highly successful *The Curious Incident of the Dog in the Night-time*, Clare Sainsbury's (2009) *Martian in the Playground*, Temple Grandin's *Emergence Labelled Autistic* or Donna Williams's (1992) *Nobody Nowhere* will provide the class with insights into the condition from an autistic perspective. Practitioners might choose to develop themes focused on literature from the field of autism.

Developing understanding of individual needs

Given the breadth of the autistic spectrum it will be necessary to develop the general information shared towards an understanding of the particular child with autism that the children know. This can be achieved by engaging the students in exercises which draw from them ideas about the difficulties faced by their classmate with autism. As indicated earlier this needs to be handled with great sensitivity and respect for the child with autism. Practitioners should be as objective as possible and avoid presenting the child as a 'curiosity'.

Suggestion box

Having taught the children about the general features of autism, present a lesson in which students are asked to:

- describe the difficulties their classmate encounters as a consequence of their autism

- record the things that they know their classmate likes and the things they dislike

- list their classmates' strengths and qualities

- suggest strategies which will support their classmates' learning.

Recognising achievement

Time should be spent identifying the achievements of people with autism and enabling the children to understand that what may seem a small step for them, is a giant leap for their classmate with autism. By attaching value to the everyday achievements of the child with autism a healthy message is shared by both the child with autism and their peers.

Deflating peer pressure

As we get older, most people desperately want to belong. Standing out is mortifying and those children who may previously have been happy to be seen as a companion for a child with an ASC may seem to reject their friends in order to protect themselves. Pre-empting this by encouraging friendship from early in children's school careers may ensure that bonds are sufficiently strong to override this period. However, on its will this is not enough; youngsters who are taking on the role of friend to a child with autism need to be supported through pastoral care and an explicit valuing of the role the youngster has adopted.

 Key points for reflection

- How would you describe your current level of knowledge and understanding of autism? What further learning opportunities would you benefit from?
- In what ways could you use the materials in the Appendix of this book to support staff development?
- Try and design a programme of learning about autism for the students in the context in which you work.

Further reading

1   Gorrod, L. (1997) *My Brother is Different: A Book for Children Who Have a Brother or Sister With Autism*. London: National Autistic Society. A child friendly and accessible explanation for children produced by the National Autistic Society.

2   Robinson, S. (2008) 'Accredited Courses in Autism'. Kidderminster: BILD. An easy-to-read table detailing courses of study published in the October 2008 edition of *Good Autism Practice*.

3   Haddon, M. (2003) *The Curious Incident of the Dog in the Night-Time.* London: Vintage Books. Whitbread Award-winning novel which takes the reader through the labyrinthine workings of the hero's mind; a compelling insight into autism.

4   Sainsbury, C. (2009) *Martian in the Playground,* 2nd edition. London, Thousand Oaks and New Delhi: SAGE. A powerful and thought-provoking story of one young person's experience of life in a confusing world.

Useful links

1   http://www.autism.org.uk/working-with/services-for-professionals/courses-for-professionals-in-autism-and-other-related-topics.aspx

2   www.bild.org.uk

Downloadable material

For downloadable materials for this chapter visit www.sagepub.co.uk/martinhanbury

Figure 3.1 Observation checklist

Addressing behavioural issues in autism

This chapter:

- Considers behavioural issues in terms of fear, flight and fight responses
- Presents proven and effective strategies for addressing each level of response
- Provides materials for planning behaviour support including a flowchart for developing risk assessment and the format for a behaviour support plan

Before we can begin to address the primary impact of autism we must develop strategies which are focused on the behavioural issues often associated with the condition. It is important to recognise that such behaviours are the result of the child's learning needs and are not themselves the learning need. Failure to appreciate this leads to the child's learning needs never being adequately addressed. However, these behavioural issues invariably present obstacles to the practitioner and therefore need to be minimised before we can get to the heart of the child's needs.

Overcoming fear

I am rationally aware that air travel is statistically far safer than any other form of transport. Nevertheless, I am scared of flying and such rationality counts for nothing when I arrive at the airport. Yet, I have developed a set of strategies to overcome my fear and so I board the plane, never happily, but I manage.

Compounded by autism, fear can appear impregnable. But it need not be and solutions lie in the same set of strategies which enable me to fly, in the same group of approaches which enable anybody to overcome their fears. These strategies need to be formed into a systematic and continuously evolving programme which is delivered consistently and skilfully across all aspects of the child's life. This systematic approach involves

- accepting

- explaining

- desensitising

- supporting

- celebrating.

Accepting

There are two components to this element of the strategy. The first of these is to consider whether we do anything at all about the fear, whether what we gain for the child is worth the undoubted anxiety we will cause him. Consult widely with parents, colleagues, fellow professionals and practitioners before embarking upon a programme. Where appropriate, include the child in these discussions. Should we decide to implement a programme, the second component comes into play. This involves us deciding which aspects of the child's behaviour we are going to accept as necessary in enabling them to overcome fear. Many children with autism have intricate and precise rituals which may well be rooted in a 'fear response'. Indeed, most human beings, most human societies, use ritual to enable them to address potentially stressful situations. Therefore, as part of the programme, we must determine which of these rituals are indispensable to the child and which are detrimental to the child's overall development. We must also consider the effect of the child's 'ritualistic behaviour' on other children in the classroom. In mainstream settings a balance must be achieved between the needs of the child with autism and the needs of the whole group. It is often necessary to explain sensitively to the class group why certain things are acceptable for the child with autism whereas they are not for other children in the group.

 Case study: Accepting

Alex returned from the summer vacation, pretty much the way Alex had been before the break. Happy, relaxed, making steady progress, comfortable with familiar people. That is, until the second Wednesday back. The taxi escort got bitten, the classroom staff were scratched and kicked. Alex cried bitterly all morning and as we set off for the swimming baths, the anxiety became palpable.

The following Wednesday Alex's mum called us before school. There had been a terrible scene at home and she was beside herself. Alex hadn't been like this for such a long time and mum had thought the bad times were over. She said, 'Do you think it's the swimming baths?' She was right. Whereas Alex had loved swimming previously, something had happened and now swimming was Hell for Alex.

For the rest of the term we tried everything we knew. There was lots of water play in school, stories about going to the baths, paddling at the poolside, reward systems, low demands, no demands. We ran out of ideas. And still every Wednesday, Alex attacked anyone who came near and cried constantly until after lunch. One Wednesday, Alex's mum called before school and said, 'Can't we just forget it?' We agreed. The gain was not worth the pain, not for Alex. Alex was unlikely to ever use the swimming baths independently, enjoyed other forms of exercise and would happily engage in these, was in good general health and only noticeably distressed on Wednesday mornings. We decided to stop swimming lessons for Alex and Wednesday mornings immediately became calmer and more productive. Alex still does not swim.

Did we do the right thing?

Explaining

It is very important to let the child with autism know what is coming next in all arenas. When asking the child to confront their anxieties we are morally obliged to inform the child exactly what is being asked of them. Given the breadth of the spectrum, the means by which this information is passed is wide ranging. However, remember that everybody's ability to process information and express ideas diminishes considerably when they are in stressful situations. How eloquent are you when a car suddenly pulls out in front of you? Therefore, be prepared with a range of materials which support the explanations you are giving to children. Support the language you use with either written instructions or pictorial systems. Be sure to present the information in small, incremental units with a clear beginning, middle and end. Crucially, maintain whatever support system you have throughout the programme, constantly reiterating for the child what is happening. The child may be encouraged to adopt the sequence of events as a mantra which they repeat as they complete the given challenge.

Same challenge, different child

This fear relates to entering the dining hall at lunchtime. In the first instance the child is an able, verbal youngster in a local primary school. In the second case, the child is a pre-verbal student in a generic severe learning difficulties (SLD) school. In both cases a visual system has been devised to explain the sequence of events to the child, one using words, the other using symbols.

1 Walk down the corridor to the dining hall.

2 You will hear noises from the hall.

3 These noises are OK. It is the other children talking or moving about.

4 Go into the hall.

5 Stand in the line for your dinner.

6 Pick up a plate from the pile.

7 Choose the things you want to eat.

8 Take your plate to your place.

9 Eat your dinner.

10 When you have finished your dinner, take your plate to the hatch.

11 You may leave the dining room and go to the library area.

12 The bell will ring at the end of break-time. You must go to class.

Figure 4.1   Same challenge, different child

Desensitising

Desensitisation is a common component of any programme enabling a person to overcome their fears. In many ways, the term is something of a misnomer because we are not aiming to remove a child's sensitivities but rather to enable the child to cope with the sensations they experience in particular situations. At the heart of this process is familiarisation. The objective is to present the child with repeated positive experiences around the issue which has been causing them anxiety. However, difficulties arise in presenting situations which do not frighten the child further and yet remain relevant to the objective of the programme. There are several tools which can be used depending on the specific child and situation being addressed. These include

- gradual introduction

- distraction techniques

- skilling up

- environmental familiarisation and

- modelling,

which may be used individually or as part of a combined programme of interventions.

Gradually introducing the child to the experience they find stressful may enable them to tolerate increasing exposure to the experience. This can be achieved across several dimensions:

1 An approach may be based around gradually increasing the amount of time a child can tolerate the experience.

2   Strategies may focus upon decreasing the physical distance a child is from the situation they find aversive.

3   An experience is broken into discrete components. The child is exposed to each of these individually and then collectively.

 Suggestion box

In this example the child is scared of school assembly. Strategies from each of the three approaches discussed above are explored.

1   The child is only required to join the group for a set amount of time, for example 3 minutes. After 3 minutes they can leave and go to a favourite place. Give the child a means of tracking time such as a small sand-timer or stopwatch. After several successful weeks at 3 minutes, increase the time to 4, then 5 minutes and so on.

2   The child sits in the corridor outside the hall. Over time, gradually move the place they sit closer to the hall door. Eventually move the place into the main hall.

3   Video a school assembly. Show the child the video over several sessions, watching a minute or two at a time. Meanwhile, take the child into the main hall when it is empty. Get them to sit on a chair in a fixed place which they are comfortable with. Expose the child to small sections of recorded applause. Gradually bring each of these components together.

Apply the principles behind these strategies to the particular area of fear you are addressing. Judging the pace at which each new element is introduced is the real test of the practitioner's skill.

Distraction techniques have served parents throughout the ages and continue to be an enduring and effective way of diverting a child's attention away from the object of fear. While these techniques are particularly useful in addressing 'one-off' difficulties such as injections or sudden thunderstorms, they have limited value when concerned with regular experiences which are part of the child's everyday life. Such experiences need to be addressed rather than circumvented and distraction techniques tend to hide issues as opposed to enabling a child to overcome them.

 Suggestion box

Always have a handy supply of things that help the child cope. Favourite toys, familiar songs or music, set conversations on favourite topics are all invaluable in one-off stressful situations. The use of these 'props' should be temporary; it is far better to work towards enabling the child to overcome their fear.

Skilling up involves teaching the child the skills they will need to overcome their fear away from the context which they associate with the fear. For example, a child who becomes scared of going into the playground because of difficulties with peers might be taught to cope with these pressures through role play or social stories. Equipped with these skills the child must then be taught to transfer these strategies to the original scenario.

Environmental permanence is a useful approach for children who may have an aversion to a particular feature which can be introduced gradually into a context in which a child is known to be secure and happy. A common use of this technique is in relation to sounds which students find aversive. These can be recorded and played very softly to the child while the child is in a 'safe place'. Gradually the volume or duration of these sounds can be increased until the child is confident when faced with this sound in its original context.

Modelling is effective where children have either particular trust of a person or a tendency to copy behaviour. It is possible to use either feature to enable the child to learn through modelling a strategy which will allow them to overcome the barrier created by their fear.

 Case study: Imran

Imran did not like swimming. But he did like Mandy. So when it came to swimming sessions, Mandy would hold his hand and stroll casually along the side of the pool, singing softly to herself. After a couple of weeks doing this, she started to dip her foot into the water every so often. The following week she knelt down and splashed her hands in the water. Imran started to copy.

The next week Mandy sat on the side dangling her feet in the pool and within a few weeks she had climbed waist-deep into the water. Imran had followed her and was soon taking the lead, becoming more and more adventurous with each passing week until he began to splash about on his own.

Supporting

This component of the programme has many and varied faces. For some students support might be overt and explicit, involving many members of staff and considerable resources. For other students it may be subtle, infrequent or casual, yet just as effective for the purpose for which it was intended. Support can come in the form of encouragement, persistence, advocacy, resources, supporting 'supporters', counselling and a host of other incarnations. However, despite this range of means and methods there are certain universal qualities which must be present for support to be effective. The first of these is that support must be thoroughly planned and tailored to the unique needs of the child. Secondly, support must be consistent and reliable and not prone to sudden, disastrous withdrawal. Finally, support must be expert, delivered by knowledgeable people with sufficient experience and continuous training.

> ## A spectrum of support
>
> The most cognitively able child with autism can experience the severest disability as a consequence of the condition. The impact of autism may not be obvious in the academic security of the classroom but may become achingly apparent during unstructured break times or when completing open ended tasks. Support for this child needs to be targeted at those times when the condition's impact is at its greatest.
>
> Other children with autism can be both severely disabled cognitively and severely impaired across the triad. These children require intensive support throughout their lives, often involving many agencies. A high level of expertise is necessary to meet the needs of these children and managers of services need to ensure sufficient support and training is available to practitioners.

Celebrating

There is a myth that children with ASC neither care about praise nor respond to positive language. It is my experience that celebrating the success of a child with ASC is just as important and just as productive as it is for any child. Furthermore, overcoming fear for any person is a major achievement; for a child with autism it is the pinnacle of endeavour. Consequently, celebrating the child's success must be an integral part of any programme targeted at overcoming their fear response. The nature of this celebration will vary according to the needs and strengths of each individual but must be based on those things that the child finds rewarding and satisfying. A well-chosen celebration of the child's achievement will reinforce the success and lead to further achievements in an ever broadening experience of the world.

Flight responses

Flight can take many forms ranging from the child physically running away from situations to the child who dominates conversations in order to avoid directed tasks and activities. However, at the heart of each form of this behaviour is the core desire to escape the situation the child finds themselves in. Strategies may vary, but the recognition that this type of behaviour fulfils a fundamental need for the child must inform any approach which is adopted. Approaches that only deal with the behaviour we 'see', will be short term and superficial in their effect. Real progress lies in removing the need for the child to escape, that is, in addressing the root cause of the behaviour. This is often very difficult because the original cause of the behaviour has disappeared under the rubble of time and can no longer be detected. The original cause can transform, so that, whereas the child originally 'escaped' because something in the room distressed them or something outside the room attracted them, the child now runs away because it is fun and stimulating to do so. Consequently, addressing the root cause of the behaviour is an exercise in archaeology, gradually peeling away layers in order understand the motives and needs of the child. This 'detective work' involves broad consultation of people in the child's life, close examination of any notes or records and targeted observations of the child in a variety of contexts. It can be lengthy and sometimes fruitless work which must be conducted with great sensitivity to both the child and other people involved with the child. It is crucial to avoid suggestions of blame or encourage unfounded speculations which may harden into unhelpful opinions.

Running away

Of the various forms of flight, this is potentially the most dangerous and presents the most immediate challenge to practitioners. Children with autism are often impulsive and usually have a very poor awareness of danger, resulting in a high risk of harm to themselves or to those attempting to rescue them. Prevention is infinitely better than cure and a thorough risk assessment is an indispensable component of practice with any child with an ASC. Always assume a 'worst case scenario', and remember that students with autism can be incredibly resourceful and alert to opportunities to escape. As we know, the best laid plans can fail and there needs to be well rehearsed contingency arrangements. Ask yourself at each stage of escape – be it out of the work area, out of the classroom, out of the school – *what will happen if...?*

The flowchart in Figure 4.2 is intended to suggest a process for developing risk assessment. Please note, the flowchart is not a risk assessment; these should be developed within the context in which you are working as each situation is unique. Risk assessment must be a dynamic process, informed by observation and analysis and responsive to changes. A risk assessment may be documented, but it is never completed.

Refusal

Refusing to engage in or complete activities can be the hardest form of behaviour for many practitioners to understand. We might well feel that we have done everything we can to make the activity accessible for the child, have judged that the child should be able to achieve success in the task, have planned scrupulously for all eventualities and yet the child refuses to engage. It appears obstinate and undermines our perception of ourselves as professionals, creating negative feelings and profound frustration. However, this form of behaviour requires as much analysis and proactive planning as those behaviour types which might more readily win our sympathy because it is rooted in those same areas of impairment which cause difficulties for the learner with autism.

Approaches towards the child's refusal to work must begin with the practitioner adjusting their mindset to a neutral setting, to the practitioner **'driving in neutral'**. In order to achieve this, try to

1   avoid being drawn into a power struggle with the child

2   focus on your objective and not the personalities involved

3   take the demands of time out of the situation – completing the task tomorrow is as valuable as completing it today

4   act as a broker between the child and the task; do not become the task!

Pre-knowledge

What do we know about the child?

- Has the child run away previously?
- Is there potential for running away again?
- Does the child have any awareness of danger?

Who do we need to contact to learn more about this child?

- Parents
- Previous provider (school, nursery, etc.)
- Other agencies (Health, SSD, etc.)

How do we use this knowledge?

Environment

What adaptations need to be made to the physical environment?

- Doors
- Windows
- Fences
- Classroom layout

Staffing

What are the implications for staffing?

- Staff: student ratio
- Staff training
- Roles/responsibilities

Observation

How are we going to learn about this child in our setting?

- Methods
- Data collection
- Analysis
- Planning

Contingency

What if the child ....

- Tries to run away?
- Is seen to run away?
- Is missing?
- Is found?

Evaluation

Has the child ....

- Been harmed?
- Been endangered?
- Changed behaviour?
- Ceased behaviour?

Figure 4.2 Flowchart for risk assessment

Photocopiable:

Educating Students on the Autistic Spectrum © Martin Hanbury, 2012 (SAGE)

Once the practitioner has separated the needs of the child from the demands of the situation, a thorough process of **investigation** into what it is about the task that is causing difficulties can begin. Break down the task into its elemental parts; include in this analysis each resource used, every part of the working environment and the teaching strategies adopted as well as the basic content of the lesson itself. Difficulties may arise from a minor component of the lesson which has immense significance for the child with autism; it may be something that we could easily replace or substitute with another element.

Give particular attention to the amount of **processing time** the child has for each element of the lesson. Much of our success or failure in teaching people with autism lies in our ability to pace lessons properly. Often refusal is caused by a child not comprehending fully what is required of them; remember for a person with autism, not understanding fully, is not understanding at all. Also remember that a child who can process information very quickly in one area, may be very poor at processing information in other areas and that the capacity to process information will vary from day to day and environment to environment.

Consider the **support materials** which could be used to enable the child to complete the task. Regardless of the child's cognitive ability, the presented task may appear overwhelming to them. Provide the child with lists of instructions, pictorial cues or a model of the end product. For many children with autism, the process of handwriting can be very difficult and painful; allow the use of computers wherever necessary. Should anybody oppose your use of supportive materials, claiming an unfair advantage to the child, remind them that as with any prosthetic, where there is a need, there should be a system of support.

 Suggestion box

Providing a model of 'closed' tasks, such as numeracy problems or scientific experiments, is comparatively straightforward. Just give an example of how a problem should be presented or how an experiment might be reported.

'Open-ended' tasks, such as creative writing or artwork, present more difficulty. Provide four or five key instructions for the task:

1   The story must contain five characters.

2   The story must take place in three different places.

3   There must be a secret in the story.

4   The story must end in a strange house.

Obsession

This aspect of the flight response is itself a defining feature of autism (Kanner 1943). In developing strategies to address this area we must give consideration to the reasons that the child is engaged in this type of behaviour. If it is to structure a confusing, muddled world, then we must apply approaches which enable the child to structure their understanding. If it is to block out unpleasant sensations, then we must either find the means to increase the child's tolerance of these sensations or remove the sensations altogether. If it is to engage in pleasurable sensations, then we must find ways of replicating these sensations via a broader range of experiences. We must also give thought as to whether we interfere at all.

While obsession is a complex area to address, there are strategies and approaches which can be employed to engage a child. These rely on our skills as practitioners to interest and motivate the learner remembering that what interests the child with autism may not be readily apparent to us. Therefore we need to take the time to observe the child, learn what it is that motivates them and, more challengingly, learn what it is about what it is that motivates them, that motivates them. Having, discovered this, we need to become skilled in the 'experience' that the child finds interesting so that we become an important resource to the child, someone who is interesting. From here we can then adapt activities to engage the child using ourselves as a conduit to the task. Become 'expert' in the child's field of interest whether it be the skills of spinning small toys or the dynasties of Ancient Egypt; become important to the child.

Understanding violent behaviour

Sadly, for some people with autism it is only when they resort to violence that their needs are met. This violence may be directed towards others, towards themselves or towards property. This behaviour, which is highly effective, becomes ingrained and therefore difficult to replace with more appropriate means of meeting needs. Often, resources are driven by crises rather than preventative intervention resulting in a demoralising cycle of events in which early indicators are ignored, preventative opportunities are missed and violent behaviour escalates. Consequently, resources are diverted from good preventative practice towards expensive, often ineffective, crisis management. Courage and foresight are needed among commissioners of services in order to end this cycle and focus on the life quality of the individuals the service is serving.

The key to this is early intervention. Inevitably, the younger the child concerned, the more likely a positive outcome. Paradoxically, it is sometimes harder to detect early warning signs with younger children as potentially violent behaviour is often dismissed as tantrums the child will grow out of. Unfortunately, for the child with a limited repertoire of skills, the chances of growing out of the behaviour, particularly if it is extremely effective, are reduced. It is therefore crucial to teach the child as early as possible, alternatives to this behaviour. Because the impact of a young child's violence is comparatively light, because the behaviour can be contained and ignored, there is the tendency for people to disregard the behaviour and fail to act. However, the continuation of this behaviour is extremely damaging for the child and the skilled intervention of adults is of paramount importance. Intervention should focus on:

- identification

- needs

- alternatives

- consistency.

The accurate and precise **identification** of the behaviour is a crucial first step. Try and be as specific as possible, avoid general comments and focus on the particular behaviour which is causing difficulty. Attempt to identify the context in which the behaviour occurs and try to quantify how often and for how long the behaviour is evident. It is as important to analyse when behaviour is not occurring as it is to identify when it is. Use this period of identification to dispel any myths which may have accumulated; common phrases such as 'He does it all the time' or 'This happens every time' need to be weighed against the facts.

Challenging behaviour is driven by **needs**. The more limited a person's options for meeting their needs, the more likely they are to develop behaviour which is challenging. Whenever we encounter challenging behaviour, the first question we must ask ourselves is 'What need is this behaviour meeting?'. Invariably, the answer to the question is a very basic need such as discomfort, stimulus, hunger, thirst, fear or loneliness. The one thing we can be certain of is that we cannot drive away the need. We can alter the behaviour which we see but we cannot change the need. We must address the need either by our own actions or by teaching the child to address the need themselves.

If we can accurately identify the need driving the behaviour, we have the opportunity to address and reduce the behaviour. The needs checklist in Figure 4.3 can be used to determine the driving force behind the child's behaviour. This can be used in this form or adapted to meet the specific circumstances the practitioner is working in.

Often practitioners find that there are several 'needs' operating simultaneously. This presents practitioners with a significant dilemma. While it is true that aiming to do 'everything' usually results in achieving 'nothing', we must also consider that in the field of challenging behaviour, the complex and shifting interplay of needs dictates that we must address several dimensions of need at the same time. There are various ways this can be done. For example, having identified the needs **frightened**, **uncomfortable**, **over-stimulated**, **angry** and **insecure** using the checklist, practitioners may grade (Figure 4.4) each component according to its influence on the behaviour. Practitioners can then decide whether they wish to:

- focus entirely on the need with the most profound influence (Figure 4.5)

- address a hierarchy of needs such as the three most influential (Figure 4.6)

- focus attention on an area of need in proportion to its influence (Figure 4.7).

When .... exhibits this behaviour is he/she

1   hungry

2   thirsty

3   frightened

4   in pain

5   uncomfortable

6   bored

7   lonely

8   over-stimulated

9   desperate for the toilet

10 anxious

11 missing somebody

12 angry

13 excited

14 sexually aroused

15 insecure

Figure 4.3   Needs checklist

 Photocopiable:
Educating Students on the Autistic Spectrum © Martin Hanbury, 2012 (SAGE)

Grade needs from 1 to 10 where the highest scores reflect the most profound influence on behaviour.

frightened	**4**
uncomfortable	**5**
over-stimulated	**8**
angry	**2**
insecure	**1**

Figure 4.4   Grading needs

Focusing solely on the dominant issue

over-stimulated	**8**

Figure 4.5   Priority

Concentrating on the three most influential areas

over-stimulated	**8**
uncomfortable	**5**
frightened	**4**

Figure 4.6   Hierarchy

Add up the values for each need. Calculate the percentage of the total represented by each figure. Dedicate that proportion of your efforts towards addressing that specific need.

Need	Grade	Percentage
frightened	**4**	**20%**
uncomfortable	**5**	**25%**
over-stimulated	**8**	**40%**
angry	**2**	**10%**
insecure	**1**	**5%**
Total	**20**	

Figure 4.7   Proportion

It is essential to remember that we cannot take away the need. Our work should focus on providing the child with **alternatives** to the behaviour in order to meet the need. Alternatives must be successful and reliable if the child is to adopt them. They must be powerful reinforcers of positive behaviour and often require us to adapt our practice in order to consistently and reliably reward positive responses.

It is useful to think of several phases of alternatives. The first phase must be easily accessible to the child, have an immediate effect and provide the child with many opportunities for 'easy success'. These early successes can provide a platform for alternatives which require the child to use newly acquired skills such as enhanced communication strategies or anger management strategies.

From this progress, alternatives can focus upon 'delaying' the reward for positive behaviour further still via the use of token systems or the celebration of 'good work'.

The following are broad examples intended only to illustrate key principles.

 ## Case study: Alternatives for Kelly

Kelly – Attacks members of staff in response to 'demand' for work. This is generally understood as an attempt to avoid the work task.

- Objective 1 – provide Kelly with an alternative way of avoiding tasks.

- Strategy 1 – teach Kelly to give a 'break' symbol to the member of staff whenever she wants to avoid work tasks. Each time Kelly attempts to hit you, block the attempt and hold up the break symbol. Encourage Kelly to begin using this symbol to obtain a break.

- Outcome 1 – this will result in Kelly using the 'break' symbol every time she wants to opt out. Initially, this will be acceptable because the symbol *has* to work.

- Objective 2 – enable Kelly to tolerate longer periods of time before break is given.

- Strategy 2 – teach Kelly to wait 10 seconds after giving 'break' symbol before she takes a break. When she gives you the symbol begin counting. Gradually build up the number of seconds you are counting for.

- Outcome 2 – Kelly will learn to delay the period of time between a behaviour and its desired effect.

- Objective 3 – Kelly to work for sustained period of time following a routine which incorporates a break at an allotted time.

- Strategy 3 – Present Kelly with a work schedule which shows the break symbol. Talk Kelly through a sequence of 'work first, then break'.

- Outcome 3 – Kelly will learn to rely on the prospect of the break coming and will tolerate increasing periods of 'demand'.

Case study: Alternatives for Josh

Josh – Bites other children during unstructured playtimes. It is generally understood that this is done to gain adult attention.

- Objective 1 – provide Josh with an alternative way of gaining adult attention.

- Strategy 1 – identified adult will focus on Josh throughout playtime, directing him into activities and engaging him in one-to-one play if Josh becomes agitated. Josh is frequently praised (three times per minute) for positive behaviour.

- Outcome 1 – other children are protected from attacks by Josh. Josh will become dependent upon adult attention for the playtime.

- Objective 2 – enable Josh to cope without adult attention for short periods of time.

- Strategy 2 – encourage Josh to play independently for up to 1 minute. Every minute praise Josh and show him you have put a tick on his 'tick chart'. At the end of the session, encourage Josh to count how many ticks he has gained.

- Outcome 2 – Josh will learn the value of positive adult attention. His dependency will be gradually reduced.

- Objective 3 – Josh will play independently for up to 5 minutes.

- Strategy 3 – Josh will be taught to come and tell an identified person that he has 'played nicely' every 5 minutes. Use a sand-timer to inform Josh of the time.

- Outcome 3 – Josh will learn to monitor his own behaviour and judge acceptable behaviour.

Having identified the behaviour, isolated the need driving the behaviour and provided the child with alternative means of addressing that need, it is vital that we achieve **consistency** across all settings in order to support the child. Consistent approaches rely upon consensus between all significant parties in the child's life with regard to the way a particular behaviour is addressed. If this is not achieved, it is unrealistic to expect everyone involved to adhere to the proposed strategy. If approaches are not consistent, it is unlikely that the child's learning will be generalised and therefore become firmly embedded. Consequently, when planning behaviour support for a child, it is crucial to involve everyone with significant input into the child's life.

It is advisable to design a written behaviour support programme in order to enable a close focus on the target behaviour and consistent approaches towards it. Plans should focus on providing alternatives to challenging behaviour through **proactive** programmes which teach skills relevant to the needs of the child (Figure 4.8). The plan should also include **active** strategies which can be used if the child is becoming anxious or distressed and help to diffuse or distract the child. If the child enters into challenging behaviour a series of planned and predictable responses, or **reactive** strategies should be employed. Across all three dimensions consistency is essential. We cannot expect the child to progress if we cannot guarantee our responses and share our expectations.

Name:	Class:	Programme:	Date:	Review:

Behaviour:

Need :

Objective:

Proactive Strategies	Active Strategies	Reactive Strategies

Written by:	Consulted:	Agreed by:

Figure 4.8 Behaviour support plan

 Photocopiable:
Educating Students on the Autistic Spectrum © Martin Hanbury, 2012 (SAGE)

Despite our best efforts to prevent violent behaviour before it becomes deeply ingrained, we may meet students for whom this behaviour has been an effective and functional form for a prolonged amount of time. It is essential that colleagues in such situations are given opportunities for accredited training in the area of behaviour support. Children with this degree of difficulty are highly complex and organisations catering for such children owe a duty of care to staff to ensure they are adequately equipped by specialists in the field to deal with such challenges. A number of established schemes are available and are best accessed via the British Institute of Learning Disability.

> ### ᘻ Key points for reflection
>
> - Reflect on the challenging behaviour presented by a child or young person with autism who you know. To what extent is that behaviour a consequence of the context in which that person lives or works?
> - Are there effective behaviour support plans in place to enable positive outcomes for the children and young people you live or work with?
> - Where could you go to seek advice or guidance around the current legislation relating to physical intervention?

Further reading

1   Hanbury, M. (2007) *Positive Behaviour Strategies to Support Children and Young People with Autism.* London, Thousand Oaks, CA and Delhi: SAGE. This book develops many of the themes and ideas explored in this chapter in greater depth.

2   Miller, L. (2009) *Practical Behaviour Management Solutions for Children and Teens with Autism: The 5P Approach.* London and Philadelphia, PA: Jessica Kingsley. This programme is a sound structured approach based on many years' practical experience in the field of autism.

3   Whitaker, P., Joy, H., Harley, J. and Edwards, D. (2001) *Challenging Behaviour and Autism: Making Sense – Making Progress.* London: National Autistic Society. An important publication from the National Autistic Society which combines expertise with a solution-focused approach.

Useful links

1   www.monacoassociates.com/

2   www.thecbf.org.uk/

3   www.bildservices.org.uk/acatalog/BILD_Publications_Catalogue

Downloadable materials

For downloadable material for this chapter please visit www.sagepub.co.uk/martinhanbury

Figure 4.2   Flowchart for risk assessment

Figure 4.3   Needs checklist

Figure 4.8   Behaviour support plan

5

Understanding the effect of the condition

> **This chapter:**
> - **Presents strategies to develop the child's understanding of the social context of the classroom**
> - **Suggests approaches to support effective communication**
> - **Discusses ways in which flexible thinking, problem solving and independence can be promoted**
> - **Offers strategies to support sensory processing**

The core deficits of autism are often obscured by a myriad of different factors. All too often, strategies are directed at superficial levels of impact of the condition without addressing these core impairments. Consequently, children do not make the progress they are capable of and become caught in an unproductive cycle of narrow learning and low expectation. For children with autism to progress well, approaches must address the fundamental impairments of autism and develop practice which is specific to the condition.

Social understanding in the classroom

How can we support the child with autism in making sense of the blurring nonsense of the classroom? First, we must identify those features of classroom society which are problematic for the student with ASC, including:

- unpredictability

- interpreting emotions

- processing time.

Some children with autism will be able to learn how to overcome some of these features via a 'remedial' curriculum (Jordan and Powell 1995); other children may need to develop skills which 'compensate' (Jordan and Powell 1995) for their inability to cope with the challenge. For example, one child may be taught to cope with a primary school assembly by gradual, carefully monitored introductions to larger and larger groups; another child may be taught a socially acceptable means of leaving the assembly when it becomes difficult for them to cope. In the first case the child's difficulties have been 'remedied', whereas in the other they have been 'compensated' for. Whatever approach is adopted, a range of strategies need to be developed for each area of difficulty for the child.

Unpredictability

This has two distinct but related dimensions, namely, the unpredictability of **people** and the unpredictability of **events**. The first of these is the hardest to legislate for; human beings are strange, unpredictable animals. Yet we can introduce controls to the classroom situation which make the behaviour of other people easier for children with ASC to predict. This should begin with you, the practitioner working with the child. Develop your practice so that as many details as possible are regular, habitual and predictable. You may need to consider facets as diverse as the clothing you wear, the materials you use with the child or the names you address colleagues by. Having ensured that your personal practice is predictable, develop consistent approaches with all colleagues. Start with those people who are in regular, direct contact with the child and spread this consistency to all members of staff. By designing a student profile (Figure 5.1) it is possible to share in an immediately accessible format the things which colleagues 'need to know' about a child; this will help promote consistency across the staff team.

While enabling colleagues to be consistent should be relatively straightforward, encouraging the child's peers to be similarly predictable is problematic, especially within a mainstream setting where practitioners will often actively encourage spontaneity and the use of initiative. However, there are ways in which this can be achieved by raising students' awareness of autism via a structured, informative programme of learning. By and large, children are unfettered by prejudice and preconception, and are able to learn in a positive and caring manner, how to support the learning needs of their peers with autism.

Structuring the day so that a predictable routine is established and reliable is at the heart of all good practice for students with autism. We know that people with autism have difficulties in organising their ideas and in perceiving order around them. Consequently, a routine becomes an absolute necessity, a prerequisite for achievement. Communicating this routine is as important as the routine itself; having a routine is no good if the child with autism doesn't know about it! The seminal work of Division TEACCH, founded in North Carolina in the late 1960s, is based on these principles of establishing a routine and communicating it effectively to the child. Further study or training in this area is highly

Name:		D.o.B	Class:	Year:	Term:

Contacts:

Communication:

Sensory processing:

Self-help skills:

Known risks:

Dietary issues:

Medical information:

Likes:	Dislikes:

Figure 5.1 Student profile

Photocopiable:

Educating Students on the Autistic Spectrum © Martin Hanbury, 2012 (SAGE)

recommended; in the meantime, ensure that your practice in the following key areas is consistent and predictable:

Language and communication – use set phrases or symbols for crucial components of the day or for activities the child finds difficult. Use a minimal amount of language when addressing potentially difficult times, remembering that the child's processing skills may be significantly diminished at these points.

Transitions – these are invariably a stressful time for children with autism and they need to be managed carefully and with skill. Give warnings of transitions and try to ensure that regular transitions such as coming into school, going to dinner or using the toilet, happen at a set time and in a set pattern.

Daily routine – establish this and ensure that you communicate it effectively to the child. This can be done in writing or by using symbols or pictures. The use of a schedule (Mesibov and Howley 2003) for children with autism would be regarded as good practice; the length of the schedule will vary according to the child's ability to project forwards in time. Define the day for the child through a series of predictable markers or milestones, that is, activities which always occur at the same time, in the same place, in the same way.

 Suggestion box

1   The start of the school day is of vital importance for children with autism. Devise an 'individual morning routine' based on the needs of the child. For some children a very low demand, minimally interactive start to the day is necessary; for others adult directed activities and a high degree of adult attention is preferred.

2   Following the individual routine, 'Greeting time' can be used to draw the child into the group using photographs to explain who is in school, symbols or words to describe what is expected during the day and music to focus the child on the information being shared.

3   Music is a fantastic resource for practitioners working with students with ASC. Music is both structured and sensory, hence its power for students with autism. Use music to start and finish activities; you may do this by playing calming music at the beginning and end of activities or you may sing songs which are familiar cues to the child.

Interpreting emotions

Learning is an emotional exercise. Students and practitioners share joy, frustration, excitement or disappointment as they strive to extend their knowledge and skills. This sharing of emotion strengthens the bond between student and practitioner, and thereby strengthens practice. Where a child has difficulty

- recognising

- understanding or

- expressing

emotional states, this bond can be impaired: therefore a significant amount of time should be devoted to addressing this difficulty. Naturally, a child's cognitive ability has an influence on the extent to which progress can be made in this area. However, the benefits of activities related to emotional development are significant and profound for all children regardless of their cognitive ability, and approaches towards this end must therefore be pursued. As indicated above, there are three chief components to this area of developmental need, each of which merits separate consideration.

Recognition

For the child with autism, this involves recognising emotions in both themselves and in other people. Once again the use of visual materials can be an effective approach for either element. While, the child's cognitive ability and level of maturity will determine the materials used, a general process of working from the self outwards, that is, recognising their own emotions before recognising those emotions in others, is generally more effective. Initially the student might focus on a narrow range of polar opposites, such as 'happy and sad', or 'like and dislike', applying these to themselves in familiar situations. From here, the range of emotions may be expanded before the child learns to interpret the emotional state of others from their facial expressions or actions. A more sophisticated range of activities might focus on inferring emotional states from contextual cues such as 'Jack cannot find his coat' or 'Emma's Mummy is poorly'. Work in this area can be supported by resources including an excellent software programme entitled 'Mindreading' by Simon Baron-Cohen.

Understanding

Understanding emotion requires a sophisticated matrix of skills which, for children with an ASC, presents many difficulties. In the context of working with children with autism, understanding emotion might be restricted to enabling the child to understand the likely causes, and probable outcomes, of an emotional state. While limited, such an approach focuses on logical conclusions rather than requiring the student to engage aspects of their comprehension which are impaired. Initially, work may focus on the *cause* of emotional states and be based in the child's immediate experiences; 'Gareth is happy because it is his birthday'. As understanding develops here, learning can progress towards appreciating the *effect* of emotional states and be based at a greater emotional distance; 'Susie was sad and did not want to talk to her friends'. Should the child show a greater degree of empathic awareness, then a more expansive programme of work can be developed, moving the child away from concrete examples and simple emotional states towards dilemmas and situations outside the child's immediate experience.

Expression

There are several components to this area of difficulty for children with autism. There are children who can be inexpressive, who show little or no emotional response when it might be expected that other people would. There are youngsters who can be inappropriately expressive, who perhaps laugh when upset or in unfortunate situations, such as at funerals. Some children with autism are excessively expressive in that they seem to overreact to emotional stimuli, laughing loudly at moderately funny things or crying profusely when mildly upset. Some children are unpredictably expressive in that at times their emotional responses seem entirely appropriate, whereas at others, their responses are inexplicable.

Our aim as practitioners is to develop not only the child's repertoire of expression but also to enable them to monitor their responses. Again the breadth of the spectrum entails that a range of strategies are necessary. For some children, the use of symbols is most appropriate, encouraging the child to express their feelings in broad, simple terms. For other children, a 'phrase book' of appropriate expressions for set situations might enable a child to comment upon their emotional state serving not only the child's needs but also our efforts to support those needs. For other children, 'social stories', presented either as written narratives (Gray 1994a) or comic strips (Gray 1994b), can provide scenarios which develop the child's understanding of appropriate modes and means of expression. This can establish a virtuous spiral wherein the child learns to manage social situations more effectively, gaining broader experience of social situations thereby further developing their social skills.

Processing time

People with autism appear to process the information they receive from the world around them in a significantly different way to other people. It is not helpful to think of this difference *quantitatively*, that is, in terms of thinking slower or faster than others, or having a greater or lesser capacity for learning, because the learning profiles of people with autism are characteristically unorthodox and uneven. It is more helpful to think of this difference in *qualitative* terms, in terms of the *way* people with autism think, the *nature* of their ability to process information. A useful metaphor for this is to visualise thought processes as a shape. Whereas most people's processing can be envisaged as a regular shape (a square, a triangle, a circle), for people with autism, irregular or abstract forms better describe the way in which their thought processes operate. In the classroom environment this presents significant problems for both the learner and the practitioner. For the child in specialist provision, these difficulties can be minimised as we learn more about the shape of their thinking and adapt the curriculum, activities and materials around them to suit their way of thinking. For the child in a mainstream classroom, the challenge is to alter a curriculum which is exclusively based on 'regular shapes', that is the conventional learner, and practice which is developed for the majority.

In either context, the skilled practitioner employs approaches which recognise the difference in processing strategies that characterise the child with autism. Practitioners need to incorporate the following features in order to support the child in processing information:

- time

- guidance

- relevant points

- small steps

- supportive materials

- silence

- re-focusing strategies.

Children with autism need **time** to absorb information and prepare a response. This aspect of their learning is not related to the child's cognitive ability, so we cannot make assumptions that the more able the child the quicker the process. People with autism do not tend to see the 'big picture' and need time in order to piece the bits of information they have into a coherent whole. In addition to this, many people with autism have difficulty in retrieving information. As a result, each time a child with autism is presented with a task, it may appear to the child that it is the first time that they have encountered this challenge. Consequently, even familiar tasks have to be re-learnt many times before they can become embedded in the child's repertoire of skills.

Children with autism will not instinctively orientate to the important information related to a task. **Guidance** can be provided in many ways depending upon the child's ability, the demands of the task and the learning context. For more able students, highlighter pens can be used to draw their attention to salient information. For children with a greater degree of learning difficulty, it is advisable to present only the necessary materials and information in order to complete the task.

Related to this feature is the need to focus the child on the **relevant points** in a task. It is important to cut out any 'background noise' which may distract the child and cause them to deviate from the task. For example, many worksheets and textbooks which are effective with students contain illustrations designed to entertain the child. A child with autism can find these extremely distracting and fixate upon a component of the presentation which has little to do with the tasks itself. Practitioners may need to adapt these materials in order to meet the needs of the child with autism. Other children, involved in elementary tasks may find the actual materials themselves distracting and fixate upon the sensory features of the equipment, distracting them from the task. In these circumstances it is necessary to consider how you might maintain the learning content of the task using different, 'neutral' materials.

In order to prevent the child becoming overwhelmed by the task, it is important to present the task as a series of **small steps**, each with a distinct beginning and ending. This will ensure the child meets with success at frequent 'milestones' along the way, encouraging them in the task and building confidence and self-esteem. For example, an able child with autism working on a series of numeracy problems might record each time he has completed a problem on a tally chart. A less able youngster, might receive a small reward each time a component of a relatively complex task is completed.

Supportive materials including written lists, symbols and pictures which focus the child on the task and constantly remind the child what is required of them are invaluable for many children with autism. Where possible, present the child with a representation of the 'end product' in order to enable them to understand what they are working towards and what it will look like when it is finished. Sometimes, the best support material available is the practitioner themselves.

It is important for practitioners to develop their practice to allow opportunities for the child to respond. For children with autism, **silence** can be golden. However, as practitioners we often verbally encourage, rephrase questions or offer helpful prompts if a child is apparently struggling to respond. This persistent encouragement could be seen as oppressive to children with autism and may add to the difficulty they are experiencing in focusing on the task. Practitioners need to make a conscious effort to leave gaps for the child to respond.

Given the many obstacles children with autism face in processing information, it is likely that they will lose sight of the original issue. Practitioners need to develop a range of **re-focusing strategies** which bring the child back to the initial challenge or task. These strategies may include scheduling the child to check the 'question' at predetermined intervals, such as every three minutes. In other situations, practitioners may decide to regularly re-focus the child on the task by verbal or gestural prompting. The difficulties faced by children with autism in processing information goes to the heart of the condition itself. Supporting children in this area requires sensitivity, knowledge of the condition and knowledge of the child.

 Suggestion box

1   Decide the key content of your lesson and write this down as bullet points.

2   Consider the least number of words you could use to deliver this key content.

3   Develop supportive materials for each phrase you plan to use.

4   Break up the content into stages of the lesson, allocating sufficient time for each phase to be delivered.

5   Decide how much time you will allow for responses before you will intervene.

6   Adjust as necessary to maintain momentum.

Supporting communication

Impairment in the area of communication is one of the defining features of autism and often its most readily noticeable characteristic. The breadth of the autistic spectrum dictates that there is a range of difficulties in this area including those children who are pre-verbal and communicate little or nothing through vocalisations, gesture and posture, to others who appear to be linguistically fluent and in command of a large vocabulary. However, throughout the whole spectrum there are distinct and pervasive problems in the area of communication and while the degree of difficulty will vary, the existence of an impairment will be universal.

Our aim as practitioners must be threefold. First, we must **identify** the communicative strategies the child uses, regardless of their current effectiveness. Secondly, we must focus on the ways in which we can **support** the child's existing communication strategies, valuing their efforts to communicate and ensuring that these efforts are productive and meaningful. Finally, we must **develop** the child's existing communication strategies further, enabling the child to increase the effectiveness of their communication.

A good starting point in this huge endeavour is to assume nothing. There is little in the behaviour of many people with autism which can conclusively and consistently inform us about their communication skills. There are people with autism who speak with apparent ease and elegance and yet cannot detect the subtleties and nuance of language, the unspoken words which account for so much of our communication. There are other people with autism who exhibit no expressive language and yet appear to comprehend the written word, while others may speak only intermittently, at times of great anxiety or in response to rare phenomena. Therefore, we can take nothing for granted and must begin our work in this area with an acknowledgement that we are moving into a complex and intriguing field.

Recognition of this, should prompt us to engage the services of specialists, namely speech and language therapists. A thorough assessment of a child's communication profile by a skilled and knowledgeable specialist is a prerequisite for effective practice with children with autism. Failure to obtain such an assessment may lead to the use of inappropriate strategies and force us into the cardinal sin of assumption. Unfortunately, locating a specialist with the time, training and tools in order to conduct meaningful assessment is rarely straightforward. As we discussed before, doing nothing is not an option, therefore practitioners need to be developing approaches which serve the needs of the child and can, when circumstances allow, be dovetailed into an evidence-based programme of intervention devised by a specialist. Speech and language therapy services can be contacted either through the local education authority or local NHS trusts.

Approaches must be based on a structured period of observation and consultation in order to determine how a child is attempting to communicate. Information should be acquired across a number of settings; children with autism invariably operate in different ways in different contexts. A variety of methods for collecting information is advisable in order to capture the complexity of the child. Video recordings of the child are particularly powerful as they enable us to spot the minutiae of the child's behaviour and identify factors which we do not always perceive when we are with the child. Interviews with parents, siblings, transport assistants, former teachers, lunchtime assistants, indeed anyone who is a part of the child's life will help build up a picture of the child's communication profile. Finally, direct observations need to be spread over a defined period of time in order to track any changes and adaptations which are occurring in the child's communicative efforts. Observations should be structured and purposeful, designed for a specific reason and take place in a variety of settings. Where possible, a number of different people using a common format should conduct the observations in order to offer different perspectives and alternative understandings.

This period of observation and consultation should be defined at the outset and not drag on aimlessly. Moreover, if suitable strategies begin to emerge at any point, then implement them; do not wait until the end of the observation period if the child will benefit from them now. Once the period is complete, a repertoire of approaches should be implemented which are underpinned by principles and understandings which are recognised as fundamental to good communication practice for people with autism.

There must be a shared acknowledgement of the 'ephemeral' nature of the spoken word. The spoken word lives for a fraction of a second then disappears. If a person finds difficulty in processing spoken language, this creates major difficulties. For the child with autism, understanding words is like trying to catch a butterfly without a butterfly net. Some children may capture the odd word or syllable, giving half-meanings, allowing partial interpretation. Others, will catch nothing that is said and grasp at the empty air for meaning.

Our challenge as practitioners is to give permanence to words. This can be achieved through three major channels. The first of these is **familiarity**, achieved by the consistent and limited use of a prescribed vocabulary in specified settings. Secondly, we can build **structure** around words, using music, rhyme or set phrases to give form to language. Finally, we can utilise the strengths many people with autism have in the visual field by employing **visual materials** to support spoken language. This can be in the form of pictures, symbols, photographs or writing depending on the individual and the context. Remember, irrespective of cognitive ability or apparent command of language, there will be some form of communication impairment and therefore the need to develop strategies to support the child's understanding and use of language.

Considering the experience of failure in communication shared by many children with autism, it is not surprising that the language environment can be aversive and threatening. None of us like doing things we are not good at and most of us avoid failure by not addressing our shortcomings. For many people with autism, the spoken word is just a barking dog, relentless, meaningless and oppressive. Ironically, the education system is populated by talkative people, skilled communicators who enjoy using language and exploring ideas through this medium. Consequently, there is the potential for a clash of cultures if practitioners are not able to adapt the use of language to the culture of the child.

Language use must be tailored to the needs of the child. It must be concrete, literal and direct. Take time to reflect on the amount of spoken language you use and then consider how much language you need to use. Is it possible to say what you need to say using fewer words? Think of the language environment as your classroom in which words are the resources and objects in your room. Just as good practice thrives in a classroom environment which is well laid out, in which resources are clearly labelled and logically arranged, so too the language environment needs to be tidy, clutter-free and above all functional. We would not leave pencils, paint pots and plasticine lying all over the room and neither should we do so with words.

Case study: From the chalkface

Lunchtimes have always been a challenge. It seems that during lunchtime we lump together everything our children are not too good at and ask them to get on with it. Not surprisingly we were having a difficult half-term settling new children into the lunchtime routine and staff were becoming downhearted.

So we did something. For a whole week, we had a member of staff sitting apart from the students and analysing the use of language in the dining hall. At the end of the week we took away the results and discussed them as a staff team. Clearly, we were using too many words and so we made a concerted effort to cut down the amount of language used in key areas.

1 Adult–adult interaction – this was discouraged unless absolutely necessary. Staff were encouraged to devise a range of 'nods and winks' in order to communicate with one another or asked to speak softly in order to obtain necessary items.

2 Child–adult interaction – this was supported entirely by visual materials and when children engaged adults in conversation they were encouraged to speak softly and for limited periods.

The effect of this change in approach was dramatic and immediate. It did not solve all our lunchtime problems; not all of these are caused by language difficulties. However it did enable us to control one factor in the lunchtime context. The atmosphere became noticeable calmer. Adults were able to identify potential difficulties more easily simply because they 'could hear themselves think'. Children became more confident in their use of language because there was less language competition. It taught us more than any other single strategy we have recently employed, how crucial it is to get the language environment right.

Children with autism do not tend to instinctively orientate to the human voice. The sound of a human has no more relevance for them than other environmental sounds; passing cars, the banging of a door, the wind rustling through leaves. Therefore, unlike most of their peers, children with autism are not tuned in the moment the speaker begins to speak. Furthermore, people with autism do not automatically know that language is referred to them. While other children are able to utilise the body language of the speaker, the context of the interaction or the intonation used in order to determine whether language is addressed to them, the child with autism cannot draw upon these instinctive cues. This results in the child apparently ignoring instructions or not responding to attempts at interactions from peers. It means that children with autism will often miss the important part of information being given because they were not aware that the information was intended for them. It is a debilitating situation to be in and leaves the child at a huge disadvantage.

Once again it is vital that the practitioner develops their practice to address the difficulties faced by the child. Many of the strategies are simple and straightforward; however, they do require us to get into good habits. The first example is simply to use the child's name at the beginning of any instruction or information being given. For example, rather than saying 'Can everybody put things away now', it is better to identify the child specifically with the instruction, saying 'Jamila listen. Jamila put things away now please' before giving the instruction to the whole class. Remember, if you say 'Put everything away now please Jamila', all Jamila is likely to hear is her name, followed by a rather confusing silence.

Another approach is to use visual cuing systems such as coloured cards to alert the child to the fact that something of significance to them is being said or symbols which ask the child to be quiet and listen. Similarly, music can be used to structure the beginning and end of sessions so that when the child hears a familiar refrain, they are aware that they need to listen for the next thing to do.

Advertisements publicising the work of the National Autistic Society have focused on the confusion caused by idiom in our use of language. Phrases such as 'eyes in the back of the head' or 'I'm all ears' are presented as examples of language use which, to the literally based child, is extremely bewildering, not to mention a little macabre! Unfortunately, practitioners are full of these sorts of maxims and sayings as they provide graphic commentary for many children and are a source of humour indicative of a strong adult–child relationship. However, they are likely to be unhelpful for many children with autism and potentially damaging to a significant few. Avoid using any such phrases and only employ humour if the child is likely to find it funny. Under no circumstances use sarcasm, irony or wit; it will be lost on the child and result in embarrassment all round.

Much of the meaning we convey in language is not carried by the words we use but rather by our posture, gesture, intonation and facial expression. These features can be as fleeting as words and are often misunderstood or just not noticed by people with autism. Furthermore, people with autism often exhibit idiosyncrasies in non-verbal communication which can, in themselves, be off-putting to others. Our aim as practitioners should be to limit the amount of confusion our posture, gesture, intonation and facial expression can cause. This invariably requires us to become less effusive, less unpredictable (and therefore probably slower and calmer in our movements) and less reliant on the frowns and smiles that are effective currency with many of the children we teach. Try only using hand movements if you are indicating something and only use pointing if you are confident the child can follow the direction of the pointer. The stiller we can become as information givers, the less complex the information the child is receiving and the more likely that the information is correctly interpreted.

Finally, whatever stratagems are employed, whatever approaches engaged, it is of paramount importance that all parties working with the child are consistent and clear in their use. This can only be achieved if the strategies are arrived at through consensus and a shared understanding both of the reason for the adoption of the approach and the way in which the approach will operate. Consultation, trust and openness are prerequisites in the drive for consistency; consistency is an absolute requirement for the development of effective communication strategies for children with autism.

Do .....

☑ Recognise and value the child's communication strategies

☑ Engage specialist support

☑ Employ visual materials to support understanding

☑ Use concrete, literal and precise language

☑ Say the child's name before any directions or instructions

☑ Be consistent

☑ Allow time for processing

Figure 5.2 Supporting communication: dos

Don't .....

☒ Make assumptions based on the child's use of language

☒ Talk too much

☒ Expect the child to know you are talking to them

☒ Use metaphor or idiom without explaining it

☒ Rely on body language and facial expression

☒ Work in isolation

Figure 5.3 Supporting communication: don'ts

Developing flexible thinking

In some respects developing flexible thinking in a child with autism is the most challenging component of a practitioner's work. We can 'see' what a child is doing in respect of communication or socialisation; we can quantify that according to a number of rating scales and plan our strategies accordingly. In the areas of communication and socialisation, we can develop approaches in line with established and credible models; we can evaluate the effect of interventions by observing external outcomes. Flexible thinking, on the other hand, is by definition internalised and hidden.

Difficulties in the ability to think flexibly affect every aspect of the child's life. The development of communication and social understanding in a child with autism is invariably hampered by the child's inability to think flexibly, creating numerous obstacles to learning. Consequently, as practitioners, it is an area of the child's learning which we must address with urgency if we are to make real progress. Developing flexible thinking in a child with autism is perhaps the most challenging area of our work, but it is also potentially the most rewarding, enduring and empowering for the child.

Naturally, the breadth of the spectrum entails that the way in which an individual child's rigidity of thought shows itself will vary. There will be children who have an extremely circumscribed repertoire of behaviours; twiddling pieces of string, flapping their hands, humming set phrases from Disney cartoons. There will be children who display highly specialised knowledge of discrete areas; experts on dinosaurs, deep sea trenches or Second World War militaria. There will be children who become hysterical if the car journey to school alters or become very angry if they are expected to do a job which is normally done by another child. Some children may 'shut down' if there are unplanned changes in their lives such as a supply teacher in class or the arrival of a new pet. Whatever the manifestation, the root cause is the same and the strategies we use as practitioners need to be developed with this impairment in mind.

Begin by trying get into the child's way of thinking. It is only by trying to understand the child's understanding that we can begin to formulate ideas about how we might develop more flexible patterns of thought. In practical terms this means starting where the child is. We know that one indicator of inflexible thinking can be seen in the child's lack of joint attention skills (Sigman et al. 1986). Many of us will have spent fruitless hours trying to draw the child into playing our games or sharing our interests; experience shows that it is far more productive to begin by joining in the child's chosen activity and then developing that activity beyond its current confines. Aim for what is **possible**; this means gradually evolving an activity around the child's existing thought patterns. Be prepared to **persevere**, it may take many months before the child shows interest in things you are doing. Once again, video-recording activities and interactions will enable you to detect some of the more fleeting moments of progress which you may otherwise miss.

Having involved yourself in what the child is doing, think of ways in which you can add another dimension to the activity. If the child twiddles string, can you introduce different types of string, different textures or colours? Can you encourage the child to use a different hand to play with the string or to share the string with you while you both play with it? If the child likes to talk about hovercrafts, can you extend the conversation to other types of transport or other types of boats? Could you learn about Christopher Cockerill or other inventions and inventors from the mid-twentieth century? How can you both extend and enhance the child's knowledge and thereby introduce more **elasticity** into the way in which the child thinks?

Another important element of practice in this area involves enabling the child with autism to better understand processes of change. It is widely acknowledged, almost to the extent of becoming a defining feature of the condition, that many people with autism do not cope well with change. This is potentially misleading. Like all of us, people with autism do not cope well with changes they cannot understand and it is this understanding which is impaired. Therefore, our efforts as practitioners should be directed towards helping the child to understand that a change is happening, why that change is happening, how it will happen and what the expected outcome will be.

In order to achieve this, it is good practice to build some element of change, something unpredictable, into the child's everyday routine. This enables the child to experience change within the secure context of their daily routine. It is advisable to ensure that these changes are small and, from your perspective, relatively insignificant – you may have to abandon the planned for change if the child reacts particularly adversely. Try altering things like the order in which you read the register, the tasks children are responsible for, the place people sit in the minibus, the circuit of activities laid out in the PE lesson. Prior to introducing the change,

- **inform** the child that there has been a change

- **explain** why this change has been made

- **predict** what will happen

- **describe** how things will turn out.

Naturally, the way in which these four points are covered will vary according to each child's needs and strengths.

Informing may take the form of verbal information, such as 'John, today there is a change. We will do Art before our numeracy session'. For other students it may be necessary to hold up a symbol showing 'Change' and drawing the child's attention to this.

Explaining change is generally difficult as change is often the result of a chain of events which cannot be easily tracked. Indeed on occasion, you may not know yourself why the school hall is out of action! Your explanation may be verbal and should begin with a clear cuing word such as 'because'. So that your conversation with John may now be: 'John, today there is a change. We will do Art before our numeracy session. This is because Mrs. Sullivan is coming in to help us with our numeracy and she cannot come until 10.30.' For other children you may have to use symbols or photographs, which will generally entail that a less sophisticated message can be conveyed. However, such devices can be used to show that something is not available or someone is absent.

Predicting what will happen during the change will help the child to overcome their fear of the unknown and give a structure to events as they unfold. Here, both language and symbols are equally effective. Pictures and symbols can provide a scheduled sequence of events, while a verbal commentary can guide the child through the expected change. Our conversation with John will now be: 'John, today there is a change. We will do Art before our numeracy session. This is because Mrs. Sullivan is coming in to help us with our numeracy and she cannot come until 10.30. We will finish our artwork by 10.15 a.m., have outside play and then line up, ready to go out of school. We are going to walk up to the road in order to carry out a traffic census similar to the one we did in April.'

Describing intended outcomes enables the child to form a mental image of what is required and therefore better understand when the change process is complete. Again images and language are equally powerful. Presenting a child with a picture of the 'final product' or telling the child how things will be different once change is complete helps to resolve the whole process. John's information is now complete: 'John, today there is a change. We will do Art before our numeracy session. This is because Mrs. Sullivan is coming in to help us with our numeracy and she cannot come until 10.30. We will finish our artwork by 10.15 a.m., have outside play and then line up, ready to go out of school. We are going to walk up to the road in order to carry out a traffic census similar to the one we did in April. When we are by the road Mrs Sullivan will help you count all the buses. You will come back to school at 11.15 and Mrs Sullivan will help you to write all about the things you found out on the computer.'

As with other aspects of practice for children with autism, presenting this information visually enhances understanding.

Planning for change in this way enables the child to not only cope with the specific change you are addressing but also to cope better with change as a concept. The child becomes accustomed to things not always adhering to set routines and learns that change does not necessarily equate to difficulties. The essential features of this approach are that it is based in a known context, populated by familiar people and is clearly explained in segmented parcels of information.

A further aspect of developing flexible thinking involves encouraging students with autism to problem solve. Opportunities may be incidental or intentional but practitioners must either seize the moment or contrive one in order to encourage the child to think adaptively and effectively. When presenting students with autism with problems to solve, an intricate balance between the support we give and freedom to fail must be found. This requires experience, professionalism and a comprehensive knowledge of the child. We must allow the child to make choices, sometimes the wrong choices, but not let them flounder in a frustrating fug. We need to encourage the child to try new things but not in such a way as to frighten them.

An effective way of achieving this is to work with the child to develop structures which enable them to problem-solve. You may discuss with the child a series of scenarios and provide them with a bullet-point list of approaches to resolving those scenarios. Initially these need to be very simple and carry a 'guarantee' of success; it is essential that the child gains confidence in their ability to work in this way. An early example might be

- If you cannot find your pencil

- Put your hand up

- When Mr. Saunders looks at you and says 'Yes Hannah' you say

- 'Mr Saunders, I can't find my pencil'

- Mr Saunders will bring a pencil to you.

This can be further developed to include incrementally more difficult challenges and less adult support. Consequently, the child will develop increasingly independent and adaptable behaviour which can be encouraged across a greater range of contexts.

For the child whose language skills would not support this approach, different challenges based on the same principles and focused on the same objectives can be introduced. For example, when setting out familiar tasks for the child, withhold particular items which the child needs. Provide the means for the child to obtain these items, such as symbols, pictures or written cue cards, but do not provide the item itself until a request is made. You may have to wait some time for the child to realise what is required; remember many children have learnt to depend on others to do everything for them. You may have to devise a cuing system to prompt the child; another adult might act as a model for requesting items.

Once this initial step has been achieved, the level of challenge can be gradually increased. Having requested the necessary item, children might not be presented with the item but told where to get the item from for themselves. Initially, this may be simply in a box on the table with the eventual objective that children locate items from storage cupboards in or near the classroom. It may be advisable, for the purposes of developing flexible thinking, to vary the place where items are stored so that the child cannot simply go to a cupboard and expect to find an item.

A final thought in this area relates to our practice and the way it may appear to the child with autism. We need to ask ourselves whether the child with autism thinks that we are inflexible thinkers. Are we rigid in the way we want things done, inflexible in our attachment to timetables or pedantic in our insistence on sameness? This is not offered to criticise the existence of regulation in our schools and classrooms but only to cause us to think about why we have such frameworks, what they do for us and how much we depend upon them. In reflecting on this we may come to a better understanding of why children with autism develop rigidities in their thinking and how, perhaps, it is not rigidity itself that presents the learner with autism with difficulty but rather the point at which that rigidity clashes with our own.

Supporting sensory processing

As our understanding of the impact of sensory processing difficulties for students with autism increases, the importance of creating an environment which is conducive to learning becomes more compelling. We know how difficult it is for anybody to work in a room which is too hot and stuffy or how it is almost impossible to concentrate effectively in noisy and hectic workplaces. Few of us work well if we are wearing clothes that are uncomfortable or are sitting on a hard chair for prolonged periods, while none of us are at our best if we feel nauseous. For students with autism, their hypo- or hyper-sensitive responses to environmental stimuli determine that they experience discomfort or distress at a markedly different threshold to their peers. Consequently, while the majority of students might be comfortable in a particular environment, the student with autism may be struggling to nullify the effects of a barrage of sensory input. Empathy with this can be found by imagining yourself working at the height of summer in an airless room, wearing shoes that are too tight while workmen are drilling holes for shelving immediately above your head.

If we do not consciously adjust the learning environment for students with autism, we are condemning them to work in intolerable conditions. We are therefore morally obliged to make the necessary adjustments and create a successful learning environment for these learners.

The specific needs of each student with autism will vary. For some students a wholesale reorganisation of the learning environment is necessary, while for others the subtlest of adjustments can have the most profound effects. Educators need to start the process of understanding the student within their environment with a thorough **assessment** of the **sensory needs** of the student combined with a **sensory audit** of the learning environment. There are a number of commercially available resources to support this exercise including Winnie Dunn's *Sensory Profile* (2008) or Olga Bogdashina's 'Sensory Profile Checklist Revised' (2003). Engaging an occupational therapist to undertake sensory profiling of students with autism represents good practice although in many areas identifying a suitably qualified professional is very difficult and the time taken to secure their services is often very lengthy. It is not realistic to expect the student to persevere in an unhelpful learning environment while support is identified and engaged. Therefore, a pragmatic solution is to encourage practitioners to undertake an initial and interim overview of needs coupled with an environmental audit based on the recognition of the need to develop a fuller and more far reaching assessment at some future time.

Having identified the fundamental sensory needs of the student, educators need to consider how they can bring about adaptations which create a more beneficial learning environment for the student. These adaptations fall into two categories, namely, those focused on the student themselves and those focused on the physical environment.

Student-focused adaptations

There are a number of tried and tested strategies which are demonstrably effective in supporting students with autism. Some of these involve using proven techniques which help regulate students' internal sensory systems, while others introduce a piece of equipment which enables students to focus in a coherent manner. Refreshingly, none of these strategies are particularly 'high-tech' or expensive; their strength lies in developing a thorough understanding of the individual's needs and the interaction between those needs and the learning environment.

One of the simplest methods for enabling students with autism to self-regulate is to introduce planned and regular **exercise breaks** into the lesson structure. These breaks may consist of a short walk around the school building or a five minute stretching session in a quiet corner of the classroom. They may involve a very intensive shuttle-run or an energy burning soft-play session. Whether it be yoga or dancercise, a regime of short, highly structured and regular breaks provide the student with the opportunity to refresh themselves and oxygenate their bloodstream. Essentially, these breaks need to be built in to the structure of the daily lesson so that they do not represent a crisis response but act as fixed anchor points in the student's learning experience. Educators need to consider what type of exercise is of most benefit to their student and determine the frequency, regularity and duration of the sessions.

In some situations, educators elect to start each school day with **sensory circuits**. These are effectively PE sessions which focus on meeting the sensory needs of the student by introducing a series of phased activities each with a specific function in sensory regulation. There are a number of ways in which sensory circuits can be structured, one of which involves three discrete stages:

1 *Alert* – the 'wake up' stage involving using physio balls, spacehoppers, trampolines for bouncing on or hoola hoops for twirling and spinning.

2 *Organisation* – this stage focuses on balance and co-ordination and involves using balance beams, throwing and catching or hopping games.

3 *Calming* – the final stage sets the conditions for the student to return to focused classroom work and can involve yoga, breathing exercises or deep pressure massage.

Specialised equipment can be purchased from a number of providers although conventional PE equipment can be used equally well for many of the activities.

Alongside these regulatory routines, there are several items which can be employed as a 'prosthetic' support to enable students to manage sensory input. It must be emphasised that effective interventions are highly personalised and what may work for one student will be useless for another. However, it is worth considering the full range of interventions in order to identify what works best for any particular student.

There are proponents of using **tinted glasses** for some students (see http://www.aspiedebi.com/) which is described as filtering out difficult wavelengths of light and therefore enabling the student to manage input to their visual channel. Some students with autism benefit significantly from wearing **ear defenders** in particular contexts in order to mitigate the effect of noisy environments. Equally, other students will use small **MP3 players** to enable them to focus effectively by feeding their auditory channel with either relaxing ambient music or in some cases white noises. While these items might seem somewhat strange in a learning environment, educators can regard these alongside any other type of aid which enables a student, including glasses for vision or hearing aids for students with a hearing impairment.

Another highly effective intervention is the use of **weighted jackets** which are of particular benefit for students with vestibular or proprioceptory difficulties. These jackets often take the form of a gillet into which weights are sewn and which can blend reasonably well into a student's school attire. Weighted jackets serve to 'centre' a student physically and, in diminishing the sensations of imbalance and discomfort, support the student's ability to concentrate for longer periods.

Adapting the physical environment

At times it may be necessary to adapt the physical environment in order to meet the needs of students with autism. This might involve wholesale, costly rebuilding and refurbishment or might involve minor alterations and adaptations to the existing fabric of the environment.

While major construction projects will be rare, any educator involved in such an initiative will benefit from researching some innovative and excellent work which has influenced the development of specialist centres for people with autism. A useful starting point can be found by reading Scottish Autism's 'Design for autism' available at http://www.scottishautism.org/autism-knowledge-services/design-for-autism/.

For most educators, low impact environmental adjustments can be extremely effective if the assessment of the student's needs and an audit of the impact of the learning environment of the student have been accurately and effectively undertaken. One of the simplest and most commonly seen elements of autism practice is the use of **screens** to create low-distraction work bases for students. These can be established in a range of contexts and might be used for differing aspects of the student's learning. The use of screens enables students with autism to filter out distracting visual and auditory stimuli and to focus on the planned learning.

Controlling the **light** within a learning space is of great importance for all students especially those with autism. Again, the needs of individual students will vary but a careful assessment will indicate to educators whether a student requires subdued or bright lighting or whether a student needs access to natural light or focused reading lamps. By using combinations of blinds, curtains, lamps and shades it is possible to create micro-environments which provide the optimal amount of lighting for the individual student.

It is equally important to manage the **acoustics** of a learning space. Given the varied design and state of repair of classrooms, this demands creative thinking from the educator. However, some basic principles can be applied notably to ensure that sound is as deadened as possible by introducing fabrics, cushions and soft furnishings wherever possible.

Finally, educators should be endeavouring to create a learning environment which is 'optimally stimulating' (Jordan and Powell 1995). Identifying what is optimal for each student requires careful assessment on an individual basis. However, the basic rules of creating a clean, uncluttered and well-ordered environment will meet many of the learning needs of students with autism and will reflect a well-organised, well-planned learning approach.

> ### Key points for reflection
>
> - Carry out a number of structured observations within your setting. What are the daily experiences of the child or young person with autism? When are they most comfortable?
> - Audit the language used in your setting. How effective is language use in supporting people with autism?
> - Explore the various sensory profiles available for supporting people with autism. Which one would be most appropriate to your environment?

Further reading

1   Cumine, V., Dunlop, J. and Stevenson, G. (2009) *Autism in the Early Years: Resource Materials for Teachers*. London: David Fulton. A highly influential contribution to the development of good practice in the early years which is child-centred and therefore enduring.

2   Gray, C. and Leigh White, A. (2002) *My Social Stories Book*. London and Philadelphia, PA: Jessica Kingsley. Part of the suite of books produced by Carol Gray offering an essential tool in the ASC toolkit.

3   Mesibov, G. and Howley, M. (2003) *Accessing the Curriculum for Students with Autistic Spectrum Disorders*. London: David Fulton. This book applies the fundamental precepts of TEACCH to the everyday classroom experience of students and practitioners.

4   Stock Kranowitz, C. (2003) *The Out-of-Sync Child Has Fun: Activities for Kids with Sensory Integration Dysfunction*. New York: Perigree. Following on from 'The Out-of-Sync Child', this book offers a wealth of advice and information in order to support people with autism in this key area.

Useful links

1   http://www.pearsonassessments.com/pai/

2   http://www.aspiedebi.com/

3   http://www.scottishautism.org/autism-knowledge-services/design-for-autism/

Downloadable material

For downloadable materials for this chapter visit www.sagepub.co.uk/martinhanbury

Figure 5.1   Student profile

6

Effective and established strategies

> **This chapter:**
>
> - **Discusses the role of assessment in planning appropriate programmes for children with autism**
> - **Provides an overview of interventions used with students with autism**
> - **Proposes the integration of a range of interventions to meet the needs of the individual learner**

There is no magic to teaching children with autism. Successful practice for students with autism is the result of sound knowledge, hard work and appropriate resources. It is an extension and refinement of many basic pedagogic principles and is attainable to those practitioners who are able to adapt their practice and remain open to learning themselves. While many people encountering students with autism for the first time will feel de-skilled and in need of a complete overhaul of their practice, it is rarely the case that this is necessary. There will be the need to adjust to the culture of autism, to moderate certain elements of practice or enhance others; but the core qualities of a good practitioner are constant and apply to teaching children across all sectors and settings.

So it is important that practitioners value themselves and their practice. It is crucial that we believe in ourselves if we want our children to believe in us. We do not expect to be right all the time or have a ready solution to every problem. But we must be secure in the knowledge that our practice and the approaches we employ are thoughtfully developed and open to improvement.

A central component of this is the need for practitioners to continuously evaluate their work and consider new ways and methods for extending their skills and knowledge. There is an abundance of interventions and approaches in the field of autism and identifying appropriate methods for individual students and contexts is seldom straightforward. The wealth of strategies available can be problematic; practitioners can be overwhelmed by the sheer number of differing, sometimes contradictory, approaches or seduced by one particular method to the exclusion of all others. As a result, the advantages of sound and effective interventions can be missed and opportunities for learning lost. Therefore, it is advisable for practitioners to develop a rationale for the approaches they select which combines an understanding of the child's learning needs and a knowledge of the theoretical and ethical basis of each approach.

As there is no magic to teaching students with autism, it is wise to treat any approach which lays claim to being a 'cure', or demands the exclusion of all other interventions, with scepticism. Autism is a lifelong condition which is manifest in as many different ways as there are individuals who experience it. Consequently, notions of a 'cure' are both insulting for those people who consider autism to be 'part of who I am' and unhelpful in restricting practice to a single approach unlikely to meet the range of needs encountered. Equally, practitioners must guard against developing practice which is too eclectic and represents a patchwork of unsuitable and half-hearted measures.

The aim must be to develop practice which integrates approaches that have been identified as appropriate into a coherent, enduring and realistic programme for the child. To arrive at this point practitioners need to exercise their skills in and knowledge of

- assessment

- interventions and approaches

- evaluation.

Each of these processes has an important role to play across all areas of life for the child with autism. However, for the purposes of this book, these terms are focused in the field of education and will not incorporate wider issues such as diagnosis, medical intervention or whole-life planning. For information regarding wider issues in the child's life refer to the National Autism Plan for Children (NIASA 2003)

Assessment

Assessing the learning needs of children with autism can be difficult and frustratingly inconclusive. Ironically, it is these very features which tell us why assessment for children with autism is so important. Because many children with autism are complex, challenging and unsuited to standard assessments, practitioners need to engage in a comprehensive programme which represents the child's learning profile, determines their level of attainment and informs the planning of appropriate future objectives.

Purpose

A key feature of meaningful assessment is **clarity of purpose**. Practitioners must have clear and well-founded objectives driving the assessment forward and defining the boundaries of the assessment process. These objectives may be seen as responses to a series of questions focusing on:

- *What* do I want to find out?

- *Why* do I want to know this?

- *How* will I obtain this information?

- *Who* will be involved?

- *When* will the process start?

- *What* will I do with the information I obtain?

Combining these answers into a coherent response enables the practitioner to develop a rationale for assessment and a clear concept of how this will directly and positively affect the child's learning.

Perspectives

Given the complexity of children with autism, meaningful assessment must be based on the principles of **triangulation**. This is a term used by map-makers, and relates to the use of measurements taken from several different reference points in order to arrive at an accurate representation of the landscape (the term is also used in social research and refers to the practice of comparing and contrasting several sets of data to check for reliability and validity). If we wish to understand the 'learning landscape' of the child with autism, we must adopt a similar strategy. Practitioners involved in the assessment of children with autism need to employ a number of perspectives in order to build up a composite assessment of the child which recognises the complexity of the learner with autism.

Practitioners need to take into account

1   **The context** – the child with autism is likely to perform in differing ways in different contexts. A meaningful assessment of the child must incorporate perspectives from the range of contexts the child experiences in order to achieve reliability and validity. It is important to bear in mind, that people comprise the context as much as the physical environment and therefore there is a need to incorporate information from a number of people in the assessment.

2   **Variable performance** – the impact of autism on the child determines that performance during the process of assessment is likely to be compromised. The 'newness' of the materials being encountered, the unfamiliarity of assessment conditions, the difficulties the child experiences in understanding what is required, are all common factors in skewing the results of assessment. However, this 'skew' is in itself important data as it shows the difficulties the child is experiencing. For example, if a child cannot perform a task in one context which he is known to be able to perform in another, this tells us something important about the barriers to learning the child encounters.

3   **Irregular learning profile** – many, if not most, children with autism have irregular learning profiles. This means that their learning neither follows orthodox

developmental pathways nor provides insights to a global view of the child's attainment. Intriguingly, many children with autism seem to achieve things that the conventional view of learning development would claim are impossible to attain without having first acquired skills the child does not appear to possess. Alternatively, these children do not have some basic skills which their level of attainment would suggest they should have. Assumptions of the child's overall ability based on evidence of their performance in specific areas are unhelpful. A child may be very able in some areas; other areas of the child's learning may be severely impaired. This disparity presents one of the greatest challenges to practitioners and determines that assessment must be based on several perspectives in order to see both the strengths and needs of the child.

4 **Well-being** – no child can be expected to perform well if they are tired, tense, ill or upset. Children with autism can be particularly prone to ill health either through associated conditions, such as epilepsy, the effect of a very restricted diet, poor sleep patterns or the consequence of living under stress for much of the time. Assessment which takes place across a range of settings and over a period of time may allow some of these issues to be evened out. It may also show that these states are enduring and influential features on the child's learning.

Methods

Having established both the purpose and perspectives of assessment, practitioners need to consider which assessment methods are going to be of most value. Methods can be characterised in several ways. There are those methods which are based on formalised, standardised approaches and those which take place under everyday, less formal situations. There are methods which are led by specialists, such as educational psychologists, occupational therapists or speech and language therapists, using specific assessment instruments. There are methods which involve parents and practitioners in an evolving dialogue of practice. Each of these has a distinct purpose and a particular value. Each of these will tell us something different about the child and deepen our understanding of his learning. Across this range, methods may involve

- observation

- interviews

- test materials

- checklists,

some of which are designed specifically for children with autism, while others are more generic to child development.

Such diversity is necessary and appropriate given the range of needs encountered on the autistic spectrum and the variety of contexts within which children, their families and practitioners operate. Our task as practitioners is to determine which combination of methods suits the purpose we have defined and offers a number of valid perspectives of the child. There are several well-established assessment tools which may help practitioners in developing their understanding of the child. Among the more common tools used in the field are the

- Psychoeducational Profile – Revised

- Early Years Observation Profile

- Assessment and Intervention Schedule

- Pre-verbal Communication Schedule

- Pragmatics Profile

- Test of Pretend Play

- Derbyshire Language Scheme

- Test for the Reception of Grammar

- Test of Ambiguity

- Sensory Profile Checklist – Revised (Olga Bogdashina)

- Sensory Profile (Winnie Dunn).

Alongside these assessments it is also useful to develop an awareness of progress from more generic measures such as

- National Curriculum levels and P levels

- Bsquared

- PIVATS

- CASPA

Which, when used in conjunction with other assessment materials, support a holistic understanding of the child or young person with autism.

However, practitioners must not underestimate the contribution of their own practice-based observations and professional insight to the assessment process. By combining formal methods, close collaboration with the child's family and the practitioner's gradually accumulated knowledge of the child, the assessment process can provide a firm foundation for the planning of an effective and relevant learning programme for the child.

The final stage in the assessment process involves determining how our understanding of the child's learning will be incorporated into the child's learning programme. It is essential at this point that the information obtained through the assessment period is shared with all relevant parties. Effective planning for children with autism is collaborative. Consequently, there must be a shared understanding of the child among everyone involved in producing the child's learning programme. This is best achieved by bringing people together at a learning planning meeting in which the assessment period is discussed and the child's future programme is considered.

 Suggestion box

At the outset of the assessment period, set a date for the learning planning meeting. Invite people with a direct input into the child's life including the child themselves where appropriate, parents and other close family members, practitioners working with the child, specialists such as speech therapists and education psychologists, social workers, care workers and health professionals. Invite people to prepare a contribution to the meeting based on their observations and assessments. For some professionals, the Data Protection Act restricts the information they are able to share; you may wish to circumvent this by consulting with parents or the young person prior to the meeting date.

Prepare some initial ideas for the child's learning programme based on your assessments. Adjust and adapt these during the meeting in the light of the information shared. Aim to have finalised the child's programme within a week of the meeting. Ensure that assessment becomes cyclical, building into your programme evaluative processes and review dates.

Interventions and approaches

Effective intervention programmes for children with autism are based upon a sound theoretical understanding of the condition supported by reputable and robust research. For the practitioner new to the field of autism, the number and range of interventions available can seem overwhelming and the apparent contradictions between approaches can be confusing. Perhaps the best advice on offer is to stick to the tried and tested both in terms of the strategies considered and the sources of information investigated. While this may seem conservative, it will save the practitioner reinventing any wheels or buying into unproven and spurious interventions. In discussing the range of treatments available, the NACP cautions

> Therapies as diverse as swimming with dolphins, being swung around in nets, dosing with evening primrose oil or listening to tapes of filtered sound have all been suggested as effective. However, recent reviews have generally indicated that many of these claims are made in the absence of any scientific data. (NIASA 2003: 88)

and this advice must prompt us all to carefully consider which approaches we adopt or endorse.

There are strategies and approaches which have worked well for many children with autism over a number of years. Within this group there is usually a way forward for the child, often by **integrating interventions** focused on the child's specific needs. Although there is no one intervention or approach that is right for all children with autism, there are features common to this core group which are known to be important to people with autism. These include:

Structure – in practice, procedures and the physical environment

Clarity – in purpose, expectations and outcomes

Consistency – across environments and between people

Modification – of practice and the environment to the culture of autism

Acceptance – of the culture of autism, its differences and strengths.

Although there is diversity among established and effective interventions, they work because they recognise the need for these components to be evident in the programme. Sometimes these features are not immediately apparent; but they will be found, to some extent, within each intervention which has a proven record for people with autism.

Structured teaching within TEACCH

The approach most widely associated with autism is known as **TEACCH** (Treatment and Education of Autistic and related Communication handicapped CHildren) which developed from the work of Eric Schopler and colleagues during the 1960s. TEACCH is a whole-life approach for people with autism that promotes the principles which underpin the **structured teaching** approach developed within the programme. These principles are based on a recognition of the characteristic strengths and impairments of people with autism. Strengths are typically:

- special interests

- rote memory skills

- visual processing

- attention to detail

- affinity for routine.

Whereas impairments are generally found in the areas of:

- verbal expression

- auditory processing

- high distractibility

- organisational skills

- generalisation of skills

- difficulty with change.

Understanding of these features evolved into the structured teaching approach used within TEACCH.

The four major components of structured teaching in the TEACCH programme are

- physical organisation

- schedules

- work systems

- task organisation (Schopler and Mesibov 1995).

In broad terms these components can be seen to represent the

- where

- when

- what

- how

of the child's learning, supporting understanding through structure, consistency and focus on the child's characteristic strengths.

The **physical organisation** relates to the layout of the classroom and other relevant learning areas, including the school hall, shared play and activity areas, toilets and bathrooms, dining areas and playgrounds. The objective is to provide clearly demarcated areas for specific activities so that the child learns to associate 'this place' with 'this activity'. These areas are signalled to the child by employing words, symbols and photographs to describe the purpose of the area. A further feature of these areas can be the use of colour to indicate a change in purpose or function for an area. For example, a table top used for group work, becomes the snack table when it is covered with a green tablecloth.

A central feature of the physical organisation of the classroom, is the use of a **transition area** (Figure 6.1). The transition area responds the difficulty people with autism have in understanding change and therefore provides an information point at which all details of change are displayed. The transition area is where **schedules** are located and where children are shown the next activity they will be involved in.

Another aspect of the physical environment relates to the **sensory stimulus** within the classroom. Children with autism generally benefit from a physical environment which is structured so as to reduce the potential for distraction or over-stimulation. This does not mean that rooms should be bare and soulless but rather that attention should be given to developing environments which are 'optimally stimulating' (Jordan and Powell 1995). Naturally this will vary from child to child and context to context; indeed in many situations, practitioners will need to balance the needs of each child in the class group in order to arrive at this point. However, for the child with autism to learn effectively, the practitioner must consider ways in which sensory

Figure 6.1 Transition area

stimuli can be diminished in order to enable the child to focus on the relevant aspects of the learning activity.

In many classrooms which accommodate children with autism, **dividers** are used to reduce visual or auditory distractions. These may be cupboards, work units or standard office dividers and are used to define a workstation for the child within which all potentially distracting elements are diminished. In autism specific environments, several such workstations may be found in a classroom; in the non-specialist setting, a single workstation may be developed within the general classroom.

For many children with autism, noise can be both highly distracting and frightening. Adopting a **low-level noise** approach is generally advisable, promoting a calm and quiet atmosphere within the classroom. In the mainstream environment this is not always easily attainable, often for the best of reasons! Where this is the case, it can be useful to encourage the child with autism to wear headphones either to muffle environmental sound or to allow them to listen to relaxing music.

Practitioners also need to consider the potential for distraction caused by noises people without autism will automatically filter out. For example, if the classroom is too near the staff car park, children may lose their focus every time an engine starts. Other children with autism will be distracted by the flow of water through the heating pipes, the barely perceptible tick of the classroom clock, the music lesson from the classroom next to yours. Some of these factors cannot be eradicated; yet with careful and creative thinking the effect of these distractions can be reduced.

We also need to be aware of sensory stimuli other than visual or auditory distractions which may impede students with autism. Many children with autism use their sense of smell to investigate items. Smells which can be pleasant to others may be strongly off-putting to a person with a heightened sensitivity in this area. Perfumes, aftershaves, soaps and shampoos can all be either over-stimulating or positively aversive to certain children. The classroom itself will consist of many smells which we may have got used to whereas the child with autism will not be able to ignore them. Thought may need to be given to glues, paints, plants and even cleaning materials used in the classroom.

Directly related to this sensory channel, is the sense of taste. Children with autism may exhibit behaviour such as mouthing or licking objects which may be inappropriate or dangerous. Some children experience a condition known as **pica** which involves the ingestion of non-edible materials and can be extremely detrimental to the child's health. On the other hand, some children are repulsed by tastes which others may find enjoyable and will therefore find places and activities associated with that taste, such as the dining room or snack table, extremely aversive.

In addition to this, many children with autism find tactile sensations very stimulating or are highly tactile defensive. Some children love to rub their hands on the surfaces of desks or chairs or sense the coolness of windows against their cheek. Others find the feel of paper horrible or the squelch of finger paint repugnant. Whatever the circumstances, whatever the sensory channel, practitioners need to eliminate those components of the environment which distract the child from purposeful and productive learning.

Another aspect of the physical organisation of the learning environment relates to the relative location of rooms and the location of items within the room. Naturally, it is common sense to locate rooms close to other environments relevant to the child's learning. For example, if a child is learning to use the toilet, it is sensible to make sure that his classroom is near to the toilet area. Or, if a child is involved in a frequent physical exercise programme, it may be helpful to place him in a classroom near to the school hall or with easy outside access. Similarly, the materials the child requires for learning must be accessible and located in a place that will not be itself distracting to the child. Over time, the distance between the child and the materials can be gradually increased in order to encourage independence, or changed in order to facilitate flexible thinking.

In developing the physical layout of the learning environment, practitioners need to think creatively and critically. For the child with autism, consideration of the physical layout of the room incorporates the obvious and the subtle, the concrete and the ambient. We need to audit the effectiveness of the learning environment's physical layout from the perspective of the child and not assume it to be effective because it resembles our concept of effective.

The second essential component of the TEACCH approach is the use of **schedules**. Schedules are a sequenced visual timetable of the events and activities of the child's day (Figure 6.2). The precise presentation of the schedule will vary in detail depending on the child's cognitive ability and experience of using schedules. For children with a limited cognitive ability, objects of reference may be used to denote the forthcoming activity, such as a toothbrush being presented to enable the child to predict it is time to clean teeth. More commonly, children may use a strip of symbols or photographs to sequence events. More able individuals will carry diaries providing written information of the expectations of the day or week or month. Whatever the presentation, the enduring principles will remain the same.

Figure 6.2 Schedules

The use of schedules is a response to the difficulties children with autism have in understanding when activities and events will take place. Schedules compensate for the problems children with autism face in spanning and sequencing time and are designed to enable the child to predict events and structure their day. Essentially, schedules organise time for children with autism without depending upon language skills which may be lacking or inconsistent. They are **visual reminders** which encourage independence by structuring time in a clear, sequential manner. As each task or activity is completed, it is removed from the schedule, showing it has passed and indicating the next task in the order. The use of the schedule can be self-motivating in that it is predictable and reliable and seems to give many children a sense of satisfaction and security.

Schedules can vary in their time span from a few seconds to extended periods. They can be used to outline the events of the school day or the sequential steps for a specified task. Presentation may be horizontal or vertical and may relate to whole-class activities, individual students or both. Schedules might be fixed to a certain point or can be transferable, carried around by the child in a 'diary-like' format. Schedules can be devised by the practitioner in conjunction with the child, allowing the development of skills in negotiation and ensuring the child understands that the schedule brings with it rewards as well as demands.

The use of schedules is a transferable skill. Once the child has become used to the concept of the schedule and has learnt to trust its structure and reliability, the schedule can be used to enable learning in a range of contexts. For example, a schedule depicting a dressing sequence can be used in the familiar context of the changing area in the school. Once the skill is established here, the schedule can be used to transfer the skill to the changing rooms in the public swimming baths or to support the child's dressing skills at home. Similarly, children who are anxious about the predictability of events outside the regular routine of school time, such as weekends or school holidays, can have schedules developed for use at home, describing the activities and events of the day.

The third key component of the TEACCH approach is the use of **work systems**. Well-designed work systems give clear information to children about what is expected of them during a task and are essential in enabling children to develop greater independence during lesson time. They teach a child to work systematically and with purpose and share the advantage of being visually based thereby avoiding any obstacles associated with the child's communication difficulties.

Within a standard TEACCH model, tasks are presented to students in boxes or trays so that the child can easily see the items they will be working with. A strip with information corresponding to the **study boxes** is placed strategically on the child's work table. The study boxes are arranged to the left of the child in the order the child will be expected to complete them which matches the corresponding information strip. This informs the child of the amount of work there is to be completed and the order in which it should be done. Crucially, the work system incorporates a **finish box**, where all completed tasks are placed. This is located to the right of the child and enables the child to see when they have completed their work. The sense of completion is important for many people with autism and work systems, like schedules, can become self-motivating, providing the child with a rewarding sense of satisfaction.

Work systems can be adapted to suit the cognitive capacity of the child. Sometimes objects might be used to match the task in the study box. Other children may use a corresponding symbol system using coloured shapes or pictures the child finds motivating such as animals, transportation or favourite cartoon characters. Some children will be able to understand and use a numerical or alphabetical system, while others will be able to read whole words describing the task they are scheduled to complete.

The final component of the TEACCH system is **task organisation**. This refers to what might be seen as instructions for completing tasks, or 'jigs' to use the terminology employed by the programme. Like other components of TEACCH, jigs can be adapted to meet the developmental needs of the individual and may range from objects which model the required end result to written instructions on how to reach the final objective of the task. Jigs are intended to encourage the child with autism to look for instructions to guide their efforts. Developing this skill has important implications for the acquisition of new skills in later life and enables the child to generalise skills to a range of settings.

An enduring feature of structured teaching is its capacity to enable people with autism to engage in learning opportunities which would otherwise be difficult for them to access. The challenge of accessing the National Curriculum for the UK has been addressed by Gary Mesibov and Marie Howley (2003) as they discuss ways in which an evolving National Curriculum and a powerful inclusion agenda can provide opportunities for the implementation of approaches focused on the needs of children with autism.

If pupils with ASC are to be successfully included it is essential that their learning needs and styles are recognised. The National Curriculum now paves the way for teachers to adopt a more flexible approach to the curriculum in relation to both appropriateness of content and methods of delivery. (Mesibov and Howley 2003: 18)

This ability to respond to changes in the general context has enabled the structured teaching methods within TEACCH to remain effective and adaptable tools for practitioners. The focus on the core strengths and needs of the learner with autism, coupled with a practicality based on real-life experiences, places TEACCH at the heart of many successful practitioners' practice.

SPELL

In the UK, best practice in the schools run by the National Autistic Society was brought together under a common framework known by the acronym SPELL. This stands for

- Structure

- Positive approaches and expectations

- Empathy

- Low arousal and

- Links,

and it is from these principles that successful strategies can be developed. The NAS describe the SPELL approach as 'the common thread running through all of the specialist services provided by the National Autistic Society' which underpins practice in all areas. Further information on this approach can be obtained through the National Autistic Society.

PECS

During the last two decades, the introduction of the Picture Exchange Communication System has made an incalculable contribution to the lives of many people with autism. PECS (Bondy and Frost 2002; Frost and Bondy 1994) is a communication system developed by Lori Frost and Andy Bondy in the 1980s based on their work with young children with autism (Frost and Bondy 2002). As with TEACCH, PECS focuses on the characteristic features of the learner with autism capitalising upon visual strengths and a capacity for learning systematically, while accommodating the difficulties caused by impairments in receiving, processing and expressing language.

PECS is incremental in its design, taking the learner through six phases, namely

- Phase One – Initiating communication

- Phase Two – Expanding the use of pictures

- Phase Three – Choosing the message within PECS

- Phase Four – Introducing the sentence structure within PECS

- Phase Five – Teaching answering simple questions

- Phase Six – Teaching commenting (Bondy and Frost 2002).

An essential feature of PECS is the **permanence** of the 'information' being exchanged. The spoken word disappears as soon as it is spoken; gesture and facial expression are similarly short-lived. For the child with autism, who takes time to process information or has difficulty accessing words or phrases, PECS provides a constant visual source of information. This supports the child's understanding and therefore promotes successful communication opportunities. As communication becomes an increasingly positive experience for the child, so the child becomes more likely to engage in positive communicative interactions, creating a virtuous spiral of successful communication.

Verbal prompts are not used in PECS. This prevents the child becoming 'prompt dependent' and encourages spontaneity in communicative efforts. PECS places the initiative for communication with the child, promoting and sustaining the motivation necessary for communication to succeed.

PECS enables the child to generalise skills to a range of contexts. This is because many of the items used in PECS are portable so that the child is able to take supportive materials from place to place and person to person. This in turn allows communication to take place in a variety of contexts. For example, a child might learn to ask for a drink in the familiar setting of his classroom, transfer this skill to the school dining room and eventually be able to request a drink in a local café or restaurant.

For many children with autism, PECS provides a successful strategy for communication. Communicative acts become effective and motivating, a positive means to a positive end for the child. For those children who do not acquire any spoken language, PECS offers an alternative to never being able to express wants and needs. For children whose language is limited, PECS can act as a scaffold which supports language development and encourages increasing language skills. For some children, PECS becomes redundant as they develop sufficient skills to no longer require the augmentation of PECS. Whatever the specific detail, the impact of PECS on the learning and lifestyle of many children with autism has been both positive and enduring.

Minimal speech approach

A minimal speech approach (Potter and Whittaker 2001) recognises the potentially aversive effect of complex language on children with autism. Therefore, the approach offers strategies for modifying the type and degree of speech used with children, focusing on key words and avoiding complex language structures.

Many children with autism rely heavily on situational clues and daily routines to enhance their understanding of language. This can create a false impression of their ability to process language, leading to an inappropriate use of language by the adults around them. Phrases such as 'Come on Terry put your coat on, the blue one, 'cause it's raining and that's got a hood on it. Oh, and remember, zip it up properly' may result in Terry putting on, and successfully zipping up, his blue raincoat. But if we analyse what Terry has actually 'processed' from this phrase it may only be the words 'coat on'. Terry may have noticed that it is raining, know from past experience that he wears his blue coat when it rains and understand he must zip it up to keep dry. When Terry appears in his zipped-up blue coat, the adult may presume that Terry associates the word and colour *blue*, knows what a *hood* is or understands what *raining* means. When these skills do not appear in other contexts, the adult may believe that Terry is being obstructive or resistant.

As a consequence of this misjudgement, far too much language is used with the child and the key words the child might have been able to process are lost in the 'noise' of words. This can lead to the child becoming anxious and opting out of using language, missing out altogether on opportunities for verbal communication.

Carol Potter and Chris Whittaker (2001) recommend the creation of a 'communication-enabling environment' through the use of the following key features:

- reducing the use of speech in all situations

- appropriate mapping of single words

- giving information in non-verbal ways

- minimising 'running commentaries'

- delaying the use of speech when teaching new tasks

- avoiding temporal terms (today, tomorrow, yesterday) as early comprehension goals.

As practitioners, our natural reaction to a child who does not understand what we are saying is to try and explain more, use more language, give more detail. However, for children with autism, less is definitely more! The reduction of language enables the child to grasp the key components of the information and focus on what is understood.

Intensive interaction

Intensive interaction is an approach pioneered by Melanie Nind and Dave Hewett which helps people with severe learning difficulties develop skills in interaction and communication (Nind and Hewett 1994; 2001). The focus on these two key areas entails that the intervention has many applications for people with autism, particularly those who also experience learning difficulties.

Intensive interaction is based on the principles of parent–baby interaction. During the first months of life, babies are frequently involved in pleasurable and rewarding interactions with adult caregivers. Adults instinctively respond to the actions of the baby, giving meaning to the baby's actions and building these actions into a familiar repertoire of activities and games. As the child develops and the interactions increase and expand, relationships are strengthened and the basis of the child's future learning is formed. If this natural, instinctive process is disrupted through the child experiencing learning difficulties or impairment, opportunities for the development of skills are restricted. Consequently, the child may not acquire the prerequisite skills for social interaction and communication. Moreover, the actions of the baby have a profound influence on the adult's response. Therefore, if the child's development is problematic, it is likely to shape the action of an adult in a way which does not promote effective interactions.

Intensive interaction aims to promote successful interactions by providing opportunities for individuals to engage in the type of reciprocal activity typical of infants and their caregivers. This includes developing an individual's understanding of the fundamentals of communication such as turn-taking, eye contact and sharing attention. This is achieved by the practitioner applying the principles of parent–baby interaction through:

- being available for interaction

- establishing a relaxed and happy ambience

- allowing the individual to take the lead

- creating space and time for responses

- giving meaning to the individual's actions and responding appropriately

- developing a familiar pattern and routine to the repertoire of actions

- extending actions and interactions.

For some people with autism, the progress made through intensive interaction has both improved the individual's quality of life and contributed to the acquisition of new skills in the areas of interaction and communication. Practitioners who develop their skills and knowledge in intensive interaction are able to apply aspects of the approach to other areas of their practice. For example, practitioners become more 'tuned in' to the child, noticing the subtle, often fleeting, cues and clues the child gives as precursors to interactive intent or readiness to respond. Importantly, practitioners who are skilled in intensive interaction are often sensitive to the amount of time a child needs to process information and judge the pauses between interactions with great skill.

Musical interaction

Another powerful intervention which has many parallels with intensive interaction is musical interaction (Prevezer 1990; Wimpory 1995). Through this approach, the difficulties children with autism have in **social timing** are addressed using music to encourage the development of pre-verbal joint attention skills.

Initially, the child's spontaneous actions and sounds are treated as intentionally communicative. The adult responds using music as a way of joining in with the child, commenting on the child's actions or shaping the activity. For example, if a child is tapping the surface of a table, the adult may join with the activity, introduce a song to the rhythm of the tapping and sing a lyric to a familiar tune which comments on the activity, such as

'Tanya taps the table top, table top, table top,

Tanya taps the table top, my fair lady ...' (to the tune of London Bridge)

The natural structures of music provide a framework for the development of critical interaction skills in the child, including:

- sharing attention

- awareness of the communicative effect of their actions

- responding to pauses

- anticipating routines.

The familiarity of favourite songs, the enjoyment of the music itself and the non-invasive nature of the approach, encourage the child to engage in interactions which they otherwise find difficult. Practitioners do not need to be music specialists to use this approach; singing or clapping rhythms are just as motivating to many children as is the skilled playing of an instrument.

The approach draws the child into interaction through a shared enjoyment of music, developing not only important communication skills but also aspects of the child's self-esteem and self-image.

Play–drama intervention

Play–drama intervention (Sherrat and Peter 2002) offers a structured approach to developing play and imagination in children with autism. The approach takes as its starting point the generally held view that children learn through their play. Play enables the child to explore, experiment and discover, it provides them with opportunities to practice and refine skills and promotes creativity, empathy and social cohesion.

However, given the fundamental impairments of autism, for many children with the condition this 'playfulness' remains latent. These problems are potentially worsened by the tendency to concentrate solely on approaches which focus on the child's relative strength in logical, sequential tasks. This narrows opportunities to exercise the child's creative and playful potential despite the fact that 'Logic would seem to suggest that children experiencing difficulty in a particular area (in this case, play) should receive more support in it, not less!' (Sherrat and Peter 2002: 3).

Dave Sherrat and Melanie Peter argue that engaging a developmental approach to play–drama intervention provides structures that enable the child to bring together logical and emotional processes which it is felt people with autism have difficulty in integrating. By bringing together the rational and creative components of their understanding, the child acquires a more 'coherent understanding'. The structures can be

gradually broadened to incorporate increasingly complex play behaviour which ulti-
mately contributes to the child's understanding of the wider world around them.

The approach identifies three key conditions for providing **purposeful play experiences** for children with autism, namely,

1   structure

2   interests

3   affect

and offers the view that children with autism need to be **enabled** and **motivated** in
order to engage in play. Fundamental to the whole process is the interaction with
'sensitive adults'.

As with other interventions, the early child–adult model of interactions which are
predictable and based on joint attention and shared meaning provide a basis for
initial activities. These are built on incrementally by rewarding 'desired' play acts
until the child is involved in play which is both complex and sophisticated. The
noticeable benefits of this approach include:

- progress in language skills

- improved social understanding

- advances in play skills to include symbolic, pretend and socio-dramatic play

- increased ability to cope with change

- reduced obsessive and repetitive behaviours

- developments in empathetic understanding

- increased spontaneity and creativity.

While the cornerstones of this approach may seem contrary to the needs of a child
experiencing the characteristic difficulties of autism, an argument can be made
for directly addressing those difficulties through a structured programme based on
sound theory robust evidence. The potential benefits of the approach must prompt
practitioners to consider how to incorporate play–drama intervention into the
child's overall learning programme.

Social stories

Social stories (Gray 1994a; 1994b; Gray and White 2002) are designed to provide
a person with autism with the social information they require to cope in a given
situation. Developed in 1991 by Carol Gray, social stories either describe situations
which are proving difficult for a person with autism or acknowledge the success and
achievement of a person with autism using a format which is both sensitive to the
perspective of the person and meaningful to them.

Social stories are described as a 'process' and a 'product'. The *process* involves the author of the story considering the situation from the perspective of the person with autism and writing a *product* using text and illustration in a way that is meaningful to the person. The story itself is specifically defined according to prescribed guidelines which define four sentence types, namely:

1   Descriptive – statements of fact

2   Perspective – describing other people's internal states

3   Affirmative – expressing generally shared values

4   Directive – identifying suggested or recommended responses.

The ratio with which these sentence types are used is also clearly prescribed with between two and five descriptive/perspective/affirmative sentences being used for each directive sentence.

The positive and sensitive nature of social stories coupled with their clear structure and individual focus enable many children with autism to overcome a range of complex and confusing situations. The permanence of the text and illustrations allow the child to revisit the story in order to consolidate developing concepts, while the simple sentence structure enables the child to memorise key phrases, mini-mantras, to recite when encountering potential difficulties.

Evaluation

Just as assessment for a child with autism is often difficult, so too is evaluating the effectiveness of interventions and approaches. This is often because of the number of variables involved in the child's life at any one time and the possible effects, good and bad, that these variables may have.

Nevertheless, we need to continuously evaluate the effectiveness of our practice and define 'milestones' at which we regularly review the child's progress. There are likely to be formal, statutory points at which this review is required; however, good practice determines the frequency with which we review a child's progress is responsive to the child's needs and the context we are working in.

The approaches described above lend themselves to continuous evaluation. They are generally incremental in design and phased in their application. Consequently, practitioners naturally arrive at points at which they consider the progress the child has made and whether they are ready for the next stage. This is a strength of these established strategies and can be used to guide practitioners through the difficult components of their practice.

As a general rule, evaluation should involve the practitioner in a series of questions asking:

•   What progress has the child made?

•   What progress had I expected the child to make?

- What factors are currently affecting the child?

- What effect have the approaches used with the child had?

- How effectively are we using these approaches?

- How skilled are we in these approaches?

- What other strategies might benefit the child?

In evaluating the progress of the child, we are invariably evaluating our own effectiveness as practitioners. For this process to be beneficial, we must be honest, fair and open to necessary change.

> ### ᗢ Key points for reflection
>
> - How can you ensure that the children or young people you are working with have access to trans-disciplinary assessments based on a holistic view of the individual? Who are your key partners in assessing individuals' needs?
> - What further research will you need to undertake in order to develop an integrated, coherent and enduring programme of interventions for the individuals you work with? What resources will you need to acquire to support the programme?
> - Consider the learning environment around you. In what ways is it equipped to support the range of interventions which might benefit children and young people with autism? Are there tensions between the environment which is 'right' for individuals with autism and other learners? How might you resolve these tensions?

Further reading

1 Bondy, A.S. and Frost, L. (2002) *A Picture's Worth: PECS and Other Visual Communication Strategies in Autism*. Bethesda: Woodbine House.

2 Mesibov, G. and Howley, M. (2003) *Accessing the Curriculum for Students with Autistic Spectrum Disorders*. London: David Fulton.

3 Nind, M. and Hewett, D. (2001) *A Practical Guide to Intensive Interaction*. Kidderminster: BILD Publications.

4 Potter, C. and Whittaker, C. (2001) *Enabling Communication in Children with Autism*. London: Jessica Kingsley.

5 Sherrat, D. and Peter, M. (2002) *Developing Play and Drama in Children with Autistic Spectrum Disorders*. London: David Fulton.

6 Wall, K. (2010) *Autism and Early Years Practice, 2nd edition*. London, Thousand Oaks, CA and Delhi: SAGE.

Useful links

1 www.teacch.com

2 www.pecs.org.uk

3 www.thegraycenter.org

Developing the curriculum for individuals with autism

This chapter:

- Considers the nature of complexity in addressing the needs of individuals with autism
- Identifies five characteristics for a new pedagogy for autism
- Proposes a structure for learning to support curriculum development
- Offers examples of curriculum development based on the structure for learning

Educators in the twenty-first century are facing an exciting and challenging project in developing a rich, meaningful and engaging curriculum for the growing numbers of learners who may be described as 'complex'. Academic research and anecdotal evidence demonstrate that the population of students with learning difficulties and disabilities is undergoing a significant and fundamental change, namely, the emergence of increasing numbers of students with complex learning difficulties and disabilities. In the words of Barry Carpenter, Director of the Specialist Schools and Academies Trust's 'Complex Learning Difficulties and Disabilities Research Project',

> there is a new breed of children with complex learning needs. The causal base of the difficulties in learning presented by these children is different from that we have traditionally known … (*Think-Piece Series for Special Education – Number 2*, http://blog.ssatrust.org.uk/thinkpiece/)

pointing us towards the absolute necessity of developing a pedagogy which meets the needs of this intriguing, enigmatic and burgeoning group of learners.

Among the broader group of learners with complex learning difficulties and disabilities are students with autism who share those features of complexity which typify students in the group and who are likely to benefit from pedagogical approaches which are rooted in an understanding of complexity. But what exactly is meant by complex learners and in what ways do complex learners differ from other learners? Perhaps an appropriate starting point for addressing these questions is to explore 'complexity' and how 'complexity' relates to the learning of students with autism.

Complexity and learning

Thinking about complexity encompasses a broad range of human activities and intellectual disciplines. Complexity theory, closely linked to Lorenz's chaos theory (1963), aims to understand the structure and behaviour of systems by examining the interrelationship and interactions between the various elements of that system. Complexity theory is applied to all manner of phenomena ranging from the Great British weather to voting patterns in general elections, from NASA's launch computer systems to animal migrations in sub-Saharan Africa. Significantly, complexity theory has a particular role to play in understanding human behaviour, notably that most compelling of all human behaviours we call learning.

As educators we are required to understand how the various elements within the student are interacting at any given time. We need to know how that student interconnects with the environment, the school community and the wider social context in which he lives. We need to understand the student as a complex system within further complex systems. In addition to this, we need to recognise our own part in the interactions that the student experiences and account for how the myriad interactions occurring within us are influencing the relationship we share with that student. As educators we are inextricably part of a series of complex and dynamic systems which we must be able to understand and work within.

Skilled and experienced educators are able to draw upon their training and expertise to navigate an understanding of this complexity and invariably achieve this to great effect. However, within complex systems there are times when interactions, interrelationships and interconnections are so subtle, so intricate and so imperfectly known that the structure and behaviour of that system remain difficult to understand and impossible to predict. Similarly, there are learners for whom the intricacy of the interactions between the various elements within them are so complex that understanding their learning remains deeply problematic for any educator. These students are those who might be described as having complex learning difficulties and disabilities (CLDD); many of these students have autism.

This relationship between complex learners and complexity theory merits deeper investigation. According to much of the literature, complexity is characterised by

1 A series or set of interacting elements

2 Dynamic, shifting relationships between each of these elements

3 Spontaneous self-organisation of these elements creating order within the system

4 A capacity for adaptation within the system in order to ensure survival

5 Uniqueness between systems

6 Progression in complexity over time,

and each of these defining characteristics can be mapped onto the common features of the complex learner. This mapping is shown in the schemata in Figure 7.1.

Complexity Theory and Complex Learners
A series or set of interacting elements
In addition to the many interacting elements that affect all students, learners with CLDD experience multiple obstacles to their learning such as serious medical problems, delayed cognitive development, sensory processing impairment and physical disability. These factors may be compounded by issues around mental health, severe social deprivation and multiple forms of discrimination.
Dynamic, shifting relationships between each of these elements
The interplay between the multiple obstacles to learning experienced by students with CLDD entails that at any given point it is impossible for the educator to identify a single point of focus for intervention. For example, the neurological disruption caused by epileptic episodes might further impair a student's cognitive development reducing the student's self-esteem and creating the conditions in which challenging behaviour emerges as a functional response.
Spontaneous self-organisation of these elements creating order within the system
Students with CLDD are invariably dependent on a reliable and well-structured routine. This can be seen as reflecting the delicate balance between internal elements operating within the individual and is particularly manifest in the desire to 'maintain sameness' found in students with autism. Often students with autism go to some lengths in order to ensure their routine is not disturbed such as following convoluted routes to given destinations or eating specific food items in a set order.
A capacity for adaptation within the system in order to ensure survival
What are often regarded as ritualised or obsessive behaviour patterns, particularly in learners with autism, may be interpreted as sophisticated adaptive survival mechanisms. In order to compensate for impairment in one area of development an individual may present exaggerated or extreme behaviour in another area. For example, a student may rock incessantly as a means of regulating sensory input thereby reducing anxiety and surviving the threat perceived through sensory distortion.
Uniqueness between systems
Just as there are no two weather systems that are the same, there are no two people that are the same. However, in the case of most human beings there are broad enough similarities for generalised principles of learning to be relevant. But, just as there are markedly complex weather systems, so too, there are markedly complex learners for whom those generalised principles are unhelpful. Students with autism vary significantly and experienced educators have to re-learn their applied skills with each individual student they encounter.
Progression in complexity over time
Experiences accumulate over time and become additional interacting elements within a person. If a person has CLDD, this accumulation of experiences may increase the complexity of their learning. For example, due to a particular catalogue of experiences a learner with CLDD may have acquired a highly specialised routine for eating which has become virtually unalterable and if disrupted results in highly challenging behaviour.

Figure 7.1   Complexity theory and complex learners

Developing our understanding of the relationship between complexity theory and complex learners drives us towards a fundamental re-evaluation of our pedagogy for these students. Just as the advent of complexity theory created a paradigm shift across a wide spectrum of intellectual disciplines so too the association of complexity theory with learning compels us to look at learning afresh. The previous orthodoxies of 'cause and effect' teaching that is *I teach effectively (cause) therefore you learn productively (effect)* can no longer be applied to a growing number of students for whom simple, singular approaches are ineffective. Complex learners require complex approaches and new challenges require a new pedagogy. The remainder of this chapter will explore how a new pedagogy might be developed for those students with CLDD who have autism.

Towards a new pedagogy

In developing a new pedagogy for students with autism it is important that we move our thinking into the domain of complexity. Consequently, it is necessary to identify a number of key principles drawn from complexity theory and align these with the effective practice which has evolved organically in many schools and colleges which cater for students with autism. The purpose in doing this is to provide a coherent theoretical context to the effective practice which can currently be found and therefore secure high-quality teaching and learning for increasing numbers of increasingly complex learners.

A new pedagogy for students with autism is characterised by five key principles, namely it is:

1   Holistic

2   Personalised

3   Trans-disciplinary

4   Technological

5   Micro-evaluative.

Holistic

Keith Morrison states that

> Complex adaptive systems comprise many *interacting* elements which must be understood together – holistically; these elements, because of their interactions, cause new elements to form and new phenomena, new structures and new rules of behaviour to occur. (2002: 12)

and it is this *understanding together* of the interconnected elements within the student which is the key to understanding students with autism. Separating out the broad range of factors impacting on the learning of student with autism may be necessary in some circumstances in order to identify a specific intervention. However, before successfully implementing that intervention, it is critical that the student is 're-assembled' so that a holistic evaluation of the consequences of that intervention is secured. There are seldom any single factors affecting the life or learning of a student with autism and it is only through holistic approaches that deep understanding and therefore effective support can be achieved.

Personalised

The variables which influence the development of any person are seemingly infinite. But over time these variables are limited by the processes of socialisation which prune and shape most individuals' behaviour into socially acceptable norms.

For people with autism, these processes are less influential in their development. Consequently, a broader, more eclectic set of variables contribute to the growth of that individual's personality and as a result, people with autism may exhibit some behaviour patterns which extend beyond social norms.

Translating this phenomenon into the classroom entails that the 'learning behaviour' of students with autism is likely to be imperfectly socialised, extend outside conventional pedagogical practice and therefore require methods which are exclusively formed around that individual's learning style. Inevitably, these approaches are highly personalised and focused on outcomes which represent success for that individual.

Trans-disciplinary

There is no single group of practitioners or professionals who are able to consistently meet the needs of the wide and varied population of students with autism. The complexity of each individual with autism coupled with the growing numbers of complex learners determines that traditional professional boundaries are not only irrelevant but have become an anachronistic obstacle to high quality education.

A new pedagogy needs to be rooted in a diverse range of disciplines drawing knowledge and understanding from discrete areas and synthesising this awareness into a coherent approach for each individual. This synthesis requires more than multidisciplinary working in which the membrane between professionals, practitioners and their discipline remains impermeable; a trans-disciplinary approach (Figure 7.2) in which contributors actively impact on one another's working practice and knowledge base provides the means by which complexity can be addressed.

Technological

In recent years technology has released a wealth of possibilities into the world of learning. For students with autism, this advance has been profound and wide-reaching, ranging from technology's contribution to our understanding of the genetic factors implicated in autism, through to a deeper understanding of the neurological characteristics associated with autism, through to practical solutions to everyday difficulties faced by people with autism.

Reflection: Trans-disciplinary Practice
A mirror is dropped onto the floor and cracks into dozens of haphazard shards. The image that mirror shows is fractured and impossible to interpret fully from one position. If each discipline takes a fixed position around the mirror they will obtain a fixed view. If each discipline reports to one another what they see, that view progresses – this is multidisciplinary working – but remains a fixed view supported by the alternative views of others. If however, each discipline moves fluidly around the mirror each discipline becomes better informed of the understanding and perspective held by others. Ultimately, this leads to a greater understanding of the image, a more holistic view.

Figure 7.2   Reflection: trans-disciplinary practice

Our new pedagogy must embrace with increasing enthusiasm the possibilities created by technological advances. This requires educators to become well informed about current medical research facilitated by technology. It also requires educators to become skilled in pragmatically discerning technologies which address the needs of learners with autism. While it is important to filter out gimmicks and gizmos, educators need to remain attuned to developments in technology and be prepared to innovate new technologically based approaches to learning.

Micro-evaluative

The more complicated a journey, the greater the need to pay close attention to the maps we are using and the direction we are taking. Complex learners of any description, including students with autism, are predictably unpredictable and their progress in learning needs to be examined on a frequent basis in a highly structured and accountable way. Where learning is unstable, educators need to introduce some element of stability, namely, a close examination of progress drawn from a holistic view of the learner.

A new pedagogy will require educators to develop new ways of ascertaining progress which is multidimensional, trans-disciplinary and based on frequent and regular 'pit-stops' for assessment and evaluation. Mapping the course towards successful outcomes for students with autism requires a micro-evaluative approach which builds gradually, incrementally and sensitively.

A structure for learning

Structuring the curriculum for learners with autism is a continuous and enthralling challenge for educators. There is a rich legacy of high-quality curriculum development across the field of autism, which is a testament to the expertise, commitment and imagination of many individual teachers, therapists, teaching assistants, psychologists and researchers. In developing the curriculum for students with autism to embrace the opportunities created by a new pedagogy, educators need to build upon this solid and enduring foundation enlivening previously latent elements of established curricula and introducing innovation to meet the needs of the twenty-first-century learner.

There are lessons that we can learn from previous experiences in this area. There have been times in the history of curriculum development when the danger of constructing a 'bolt-on' curriculum has been a constant threat. For example, the implementation of the National Curriculum engendered a climate in which educators had to be very careful not to produce a curriculum for learners with autism which was an appendix to the 'real curriculum' that was followed by other learners. The demands of centrally imposed curriculum projects have challenged educators in the field of autism because these initiatives are based on a perception of the needs of the majority of learners and are never focused on the learning needs or strengths of the minority learner with autism. The repeated failure of curriculum authorities to produce a truly inclusive curriculum structured around a truly inclusive pedagogy has hindered the development of a curriculum for students with autism which both recognised their entitlement to a breadth of learning opportunities and focused on their specific needs as a group of learners. Therefore educators in the field of autism must seize the opportunity presented by a growing awareness of autism coupled with a strong legacy of excellence to create exciting new schemes of learning for students with autism across all learning contexts.

In developing the curriculum for students with autism, it is helpful to consider key features which characterise effective curriculum models. While models may vary from setting to setting, the common elements which recur regardless of the context are that the curriculum has

1 Rationale

2 Structure

3 Relevance

4 Flexibility

5 Realism

6 Aspiration

Rationale

Underpinning every effective curriculum for students with autism is a strong rationale, a clear reason for 'doing what we are doing'. In many cases this rationale is developed by a broad cross-section of the learning community working together over time to identify the core purpose of the curriculum. Consequently, there is a shared sense of ownership around the curriculum and a commitment to delivering a curriculum that all parties have signed up for.

Structure

An effective curriculum for any learner is built upon a concept of the fundamental building blocks for learning and a clear sighted route for progression. For students with autism these axioms are doubly important and yet doubly difficult to achieve. The foundations of learning for many students with autism do not seem to adhere to generalised principles and notions of progression are often highly unorthodox. In order to address this conundrum, effective curriculum models for students with autism are based upon high-quality assessment for learning which supports an understanding of the individual's learning profile. From this a personalised learning programme within the context of a structured curriculum can be developed.

Relevance

For students to be engaged in any learning, both the content and the delivery of that learning must be relevant to them. Effective curriculum models for students with autism combine both a highly motivating menu of learning and a range of autism specific approaches which engage and captivate the learner. In developing the curriculum for students with autism, *what* we do and *how* we do it are mutually dependent and of equal importance.

Flexibility

The great skill in developing an effective curriculum for students with autism lies in combining the axiomatic need for structure with the equally compelling need for flexibility. The learning of students with autism may be impacted by such a broad array of variables that the student's capacity for learning may alter from day to day; more commonly students with autism will experience periods of time during which their learning is significantly disrupted by any number of factors. During these periods, educators need to be flexible in the delivery of learning and adjust to the instability the student is experiencing by providing an assured yet adaptable programme for learning.

Realism

The autism spectrum represents a fascinating breadth of cognitive ability and learning style. Therefore conventional measures of expectations for learning outcomes are of limited value to the educator and a new set of values needs to be developed for each learner based on comprehensive multidimensional assessment, effective and accurate tracking of student progress and sophisticated processes for profiling expected outcomes for learners.

Aspiration

Closely related to the need for realistic expectations is the equally important need to develop a culture of aspiration around each student with autism. Once again strong systems for recognising each student's potential are crucial in developing this culture. Equally a paradigm shift among educators in what is aspired to is vital. Success can no longer be judged solely by linear attainment but must embrace a recognition of individual worth and personal aspiration.

These key characteristics present continuity in curriculum development, providing a link between the high-quality curriculum models currently in place and the future models which the twenty-first-century student with autism will require. Future curriculum models will require these features to be in place if they are to effectively meet the needs of students with autism and it may be useful for schools and other learning organisations to undertake an evaluation of their capacity to develop a twenty-first-century curriculum for learners with autism.

Figure 7.3 offers an opportunity for practitioners to chart their current curriculum provision against the six key characteristics identified previously. The process involves one or more people making a judgement about their current provision against a continuum within which '0' represents a severe short-coming in this area while '10' represents exemplary practice. Each discrete area can be graded individually and then an overall score obtained in order to judge the capacity of their current curriculum model to provide for increasingly complex learners. Schools can then plan ways in which they can further develop their curriculum provision by focusing either on distinct areas or on their overall score.

The double helix curriculum model

There are a number of ways in which we might construct a model for developing the curriculum for students with autism. As previously discussed, it is important to avoid the 'bolt-on' model or the 'appendix' model in which a hierarchical dynamic is created between the 'important learning' of the main curriculum and the 'autism learning' of an 'autism curriculum'. Crucially, in developing the curriculum for students with autism educators should be exploring ways in which an inclusive curriculum interweaves the entitlement all learners have for a rich and fulfilling learning

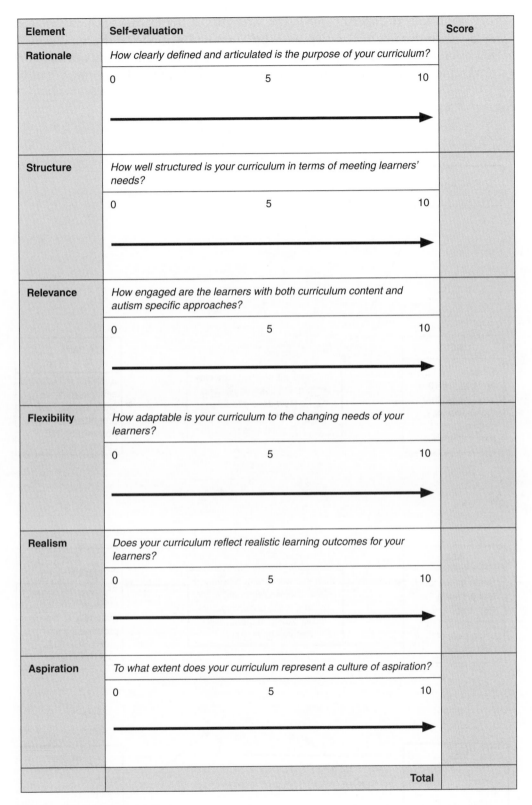

Element	Self-evaluation	Score
Rationale	*How clearly defined and articulated is the purpose of your curriculum?* 0　　　　　　　5　　　　　　　10	
Structure	*How well structured is your curriculum in terms of meeting learners' needs?* 0　　　　　　　5　　　　　　　10	
Relevance	*How engaged are the learners with both curriculum content and autism specific approaches?* 0　　　　　　　5　　　　　　　10	
Flexibility	*How adaptable is your curriculum to the changing needs of your learners?* 0　　　　　　　5　　　　　　　10	
Realism	*Does your curriculum reflect realistic learning outcomes for your learners?* 0　　　　　　　5　　　　　　　10	
Aspiration	*To what extent does your curriculum represent a culture of aspiration?* 0　　　　　　　5　　　　　　　10	
		Total

Figure 7.3　Self-evaluation

Photocopiable:

Educating Students on the Autistic Spectrum © Martin Hanbury, 2012 (SAGE)

programme with the specific needs and strengths of the learner with autism. One way in which this might be visualised is by adopting the model of the 'double helix' (Figure 7.4) for which one strand represents a rich and varied learning offer and one strand represents autism specific learning content and approaches.

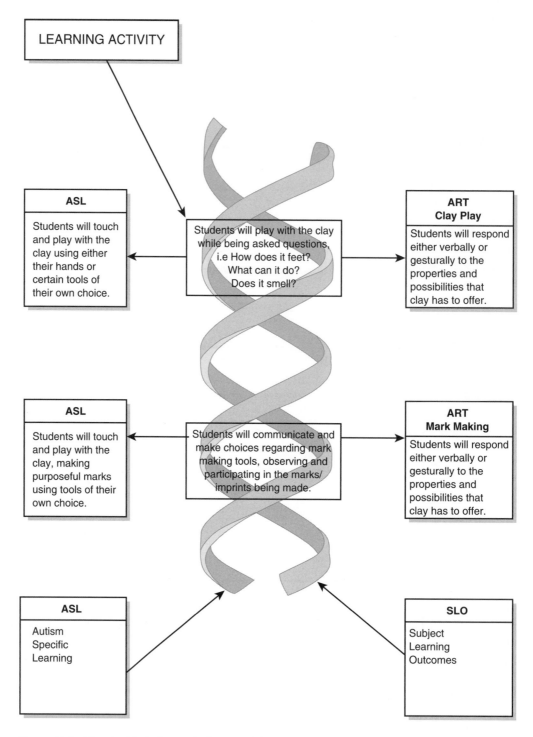

Figure 7.4 The double helix curriculum model

An essential feature of this curriculum model is that the autism specific element of the curriculum is not separated from other components of the curriculum but is interwoven with all aspects of a student's learning. The linkage between the various elements of a student's learning are established at the outset of the curriculum development exercise with activities identified which address both autism specific aspects of learning and more orthodox curriculum content. These are the steps through which the student progresses on their learning journey.

The double helix model supports the development of a curriculum which responds to complexity in learning and the requirements of a new pedagogy. The model does not separate curriculum content into silos of learning or divide teaching methods and approaches from subject matter. Instead, the double helix interweaves orthodox curriculum content and the need to incorporate specific learning experiences and approaches for students with autism thereby linking all elements of learning. It therefore offers a *holistic* framework within which the various *interacting elements* at play in the learning of students with autism are understood.

The framework can be *adapted* to the strengths and needs of the student, providing a highly *personalised* learning programme for each individual. This enables the programme for each student to address their *unique* qualities and characteristics within the context of a shared curriculum. Equally, the model's spiral construction enables it to be highly responsive to the *dynamic*, shifting pattern of learning needs experienced by many students with autism. The fine adjustments possible within this model support a *micro-evaluative* approach to understanding the learning of students based on a *trans-disciplinary* ethos which ensures that progression is maintained at all times.

Crucially the double helix curriculum model is a flexible structure which can be developed to meet the specific context within which a student with autism is learning. For example, the composition of the strands can be adapted by the educator to reflect the needs of the learner in a mainstream classroom, a resourced provision or a special school. Therefore one strand might represent a single subject area, such as English or mathematics, while the other strand might represent autism specific learning areas such as flexibility of thought or social understanding. The links between the two strands of the helix are provided by a single activity which addresses both aspects of a student's learning. This is represented in a simplified tabular form in Figure 7.5.

The examples in Figures 7.6, 7.7 and 7.8 show the concept of the double helix transferred to a simple format for planning purposes. The columns on the left and right represent the interwoven strands, while the central column marked 'Learning Activity' represents the linkage between the strands achieved through the practitioner's choice of activity.

While these examples represent just three curriculum areas and are limited in their scope, they serve to illustrate several important features of the model. In the first instance, it is important to note that the notion of 'progression' shown on the right-hand side of the figure does not express simple linear forms of progress; this would not be appropriate for students with autism. Therefore the learning outcomes shown in the blocks in the subject focus column (English, mathematics or science) do not necessarily follow an orthodox sequence of learning that might be found in other schemes of work. It is crucial that progression is secured and that learning does not stagnate around a restricted set of skills; it is equally important

Autism specific Learning	Learning Activity	Subject Area Focus	PROGRESSION
	Single activity links across both aspects of students' learning ←——————→		

Figure 7.5   Linking the strands

Autism specific Learning	Learning Activity	English	PROGRESSION
Students socially engage with adult and peers (Social understanding)	Students share a book with a familiar adult and then read out the story to the whole class	To read six or more high frequency words; *is, a, in, on, it, I*	
Students' vestibular and proprioceptive system stimulated during activity (Sensory processing)	Write high frequency words on the white balls in the ball pool Throw the ball to the student and encourage them to read the word	To recognise six or more high frequency words; *is, a, in, on, it, I*	
Students share stories with peers (Social understanding)	Group reading exercise in which students verbalise or use PECS and/or Makaton to predict the next word in familiar stories	To predict words or symbols during shared reading	
Students are socially aware of others in the class (Social understanding) Students use PECS to communicate and comment with an adult (Social communication)	Students perform a role in front of the class such as *sweeping, drying plate, pouring water.* Peers to comment on what the student is doing. Support using PECS	To comment on the actions of others	
Student comments to another person using PECS (Social communication)	Students use the PECS sentence structure, 'I can see …' Students comment on presented photographs. Use photographs that are motivating to the student	To make comments about stories or events presented in a photographic form	
Students respond to another person's attempts to communicate (Social communication)	Share text or pictures with a student asking another student questions about the item such as *'where is John?' 'what colour is the bird?'* etc.	To respond either verbally or gesturally to questions about a shared text or picture	

Figure 7.6   Planning template: English

Autism specific Learning	Learning Activity	Mathematics	P
Student answers independently using speech or symbol (Social communication)	Present series of different word problems using terms 'add' 'altogether' 'more' 'take away' 'leave' 'how many are left'. Use sand collages to support understanding	To respond appropriately to the terms 'add' 'altogether' 'more' 'take away' 'leave' 'how many are left'	R O G
Student is able to solve problems with fading adult support (Flexibility of thought)	Present simple written word problems. Use PECS to support understanding of problems. Students to record data using pictures	To solve simple word problems using the terms 'addition' and 'subtraction'	R E S
Student accepts that it is OK to make mistakes or get things wrong (Flexibility of thought)	Present estimation exercises including 'which set has got more/less?' and 'what might happen if …?'	To make accurate estimations of amounts focusing on concepts of 'more' and 'less'	S I O
Student takes turns and shows interest in what others are doing (Social understanding)	Introduce number square to indicate 1 more/less than a given number. Extend to 2 more/less	To add 1 more to a set and accurately count how many. To take 1 away from a set and count how many	N
Student tolerates working across different class groups. (Social understanding)	Practical exercise visiting other class groups to count how many students altogether across the two groups. 'How many people are in this group from class 1? How many from class 2? How many altogether?'	To understand addition as the combination of 2 groups	

Figure 7.7   Planning template: Mathematics

Autism specific Learning	Learning Activity	Science	P
Students turn take in exploration of favoured items or objects (Social understanding)	Students working in pairs select favoured items or objects and then take turns in exploring favoured item or object	To select preferred items or objects	R O
Students express preference for specific item or object (Social communication)	Students presented with flower or herb one at a time. Student to press Big Mac to express like or dislike	To express like/dislike for a given item or object	G R E
Students express interest in materials by exploring objects (Social communication)	Present range of previously encountered flowers and herbs. Students to select object they wish to explore	To show intentional communication by reaching or gesturing towards materials they want to explore	S S I
Students demonstrate readiness for learning and interacting (Sensory processing)	A range of smelling activities related to flowers and herbs. Students' likes/dislikes noted by staff from expression/reaction	To make responses to different living things	O N
Students able to work across different learning environments (Flexibility of thought)	Students visit sensory garden and explore flowers and herbs. Range of flowers and herbs picked and brought into classroom setting	To become familiar with sensations in outdoor and indoor settings	

Figure 7.8   Planning template: Science

Autism specific Learning	Learning Activity	Subject Area Focus	P R O G R E S S I O N
Autism specific target relates to specific feature of autism such as Triad of Impairment or Sensory Processing	Single activity links across both aspects of students' learning	Learning outcome referenced to 'P level' or National Curriculum level	

Figure 7.9   Holistic learning programme

to ensure that learning weaves around the needs of the learner and adopts a flexible and responsive route towards success. By referencing the 'P level' or National Curriculum level associated with the learning outcome they have identified, practitioners can ensure that progress is maintained without having to follow a rigid and therefore ineffective learning sequence.

Similarly, autism specific learning objectives need to focus on those features which need to be developed in order to enable students to progress in their learning. It is important to ensure that objectives in this area are not seen simply as ends in themselves but as part of a holistic programme of learning (Figure 7.9).

Finally, these examples show English, mathematics and science as the subject focus for planning. However, the model can be adapted to whatever suits the learning context or learning focus of the practitioner. Therefore, the model can be used across all phases and sectors, and be adapted to either narrow subject-specific objectives or broad thematic projects. It can be used for whole-class groupings or for individual students working within a large class group. It could be used to plan a very time limited initiative with a student or as used to map out learning over a whole school year. Whatever purpose the model is put to, it is critical to maintain the notion of interwoven planning providing a holistic programme of learning for the individual.

Conclusion

In developing a curriculum for students with autism, educators are embarking on an exciting and yet challenging learning journey. We cannot undertake this journey alone – it is too complex and too demanding. The work of many progressive learning organisations and the gathering legislative framework outlined in the UK by the special educational needs Green Paper, *Support and Aspiration* (DFE 2011), point the way clearly towards a future framed by collaborative practice.

This is a future we must endeavour not only to be part of but to shape. To this end, we must work increasingly closely with students, their families and fellow practitioners to develop a new pedagogy based on innovative curriculum design which meets the needs of the growing number of learners with an increasingly complex learning profile.

Key points for reflection

- Have you noted changes in the student population in your setting? If so, how would you characterise this?
- Conduct a self-evaluation of your curriculum provision using the table provided. What does it tell you about your current provision? How might you look to develop your curriculum?
- How would you characterise the trans-disciplinary practice in your school? What collaborations are deeply embedded in your day-to-day practice?

Further reading

1   Morrison, K. (2002) *School Leadership and Complexity Theory.* London: RoutledgeFalmer.

2   Department for Education (2011) *Support and Aspiration: A New Approach to Special Educational Needs and Disability.* London: HMSO.

Useful links

1   http://blog.ssatrust.org.uk

2   http://www.education.gov.uk/publications/eOrderingDownload/Green-Paper-SEN.pdf

Downloadable material

For downloadable materials for this chapter visit www.sagepub.co.uk/martinhanbury

Figure 7.3   Self-evaluation

Epilogue

In putting together the second edition of this book it has become ever clearer to me that our duty as practitioners is to be constantly seeking to evolve and adapt to an ever-changing learning context. The students we teach, the colleagues we work alongside, the legislation we are operating under and our knowledge of learning are in a constant state of flux. Against this backdrop of change the only thing we can remain sure of is the need to change ourselves by better understanding the people we work with and sharing that understanding with colleagues and families.

We have come a long way in a short time which is a testament to how the field is growing and learning together. Long may it continue as there is a long way to go.

Martin Hanbury

Appendix: INSET materials

Developing Practice for the Student with Autism

Aims:

1 To develop understanding of autism
2 To consider learning needs based on this understanding
3 To apply this knowledge to the working context
4 To customise this knowledge to particular contexts

Objective	Activity	Process	Resources	Time
To determine participants' existing understanding of autism.	Participants to write down what the term 'autism' means to them. Colleagues then feed back description to whole group.	Have people complete this exercise individually, without discussion. You are after initial impressions so only allow a minute or so for the description.	Pen and paper	15 minutes
Pause: Responses to this activity will provide you with an early impression of people's understanding. Time spent in discussing the definition presented in the next activity can be adjusted to meet the needs of participants. It is important that an accurate and valid understanding of the condition is shared by all participants as early as possible in the training.				
To provide a definition of autism based on established knowledge.	Trainer to provide definition of autism drawn from literature. Discuss the definition. Encourage people to relate this definition to the students they work with.	Use visual materials to show the definition.	Slide 1	15 minutes
To inform participants of current conceptual models of autism.	Trainer to review • Triad of impairments • Mind-blindness • Central coherence • Executive function • Sensory processing	Trainer to present models using visual materials. Provide written descriptions of each model for use in next activity.	Slides 2–6	60 minutes

(Continued)

(Continued)

Pause: This has been a whistle-stop tour of autism! Ensure that participants have references to further their knowledge if they wish to.

To encourage participants to consider the impact of autism on a child's learning.	Group activity in which each group focuses on a model and lists how the features of that model will impact on a person's learning.	Form groups, give out descriptors of models. Group to list as many ways as they can think of in which the model impacts on learning. Follow by each group presenting this to whole group. Discussion.	Flipchart paper, markers	60 minutes
To enable participants to identify features of their current practice that might present obstacles to learning for a child with autism.	Individuals to reflect on their practice focusing on the obstacles to learning for a child with ASC in their classroom.	Have people complete this exercise individually, without discussion. Maintain this as a 'private' exercise.	Pen and paper	15 minutes
To inform participants of effective interventions for students with autism.	Trainer to review • TEACCH • PECS	Trainer to present interventions using visual materials.	Slides 7 and 8	60 minutes
To encourage participants to apply information in order to address the learning needs of students with autism.	Groups to devise realistic classroom scenarios identifying 3–5 obstacles to learning for students with ASC. Groups to nominate strategies and means for implementing them in order to overcome these obstacles. Present for whole-group discussion.	Form groups; provide support where necessary, offering scenarios, providing concrete examples of difficulties. Allow 10 minutes. Move group on to problem solving section. Allow 30 minutes. Encourage in-depth discussion of each issue. Final plenary; each group to present.	Flipchart, pens	60 minutes
To reflect on learning achieved.	Each member of group to identify one issue they will take away from the session.	Open discussion. Move round each group member. Encourage differing responses.		15 minutes

Slide 1

What is autism?

1 Autism spectrum condition is the term used to describe a range of behaviourally defined neurodevelopmental conditions.

2 They are characterised by impairments in

- Social interaction

- Social communication and language development

- A restricted repertoire of interests, behaviours and activities.

3 Sensory abnormalities and unusual interest in some sensations are common.

4 A lack of imaginative play indicates an underlying difficulty with generation of ideas that is highly relevant in the development of understanding of other people and other situations.

5 All of these characteristics can be seen in varying degrees of severity.

6 As a developmental condition, the manifestation of autism for any one individual will vary

- across the lifespan

- with maturation

- according to the effects of different environments

- due to specific interventions and treatments.

Source: Charman and Care (2004)

Slide 2

The triad of impairments (Wing and Gould 1979).

- Social interaction

- Social communication and

- Imagination

'we found that all children with "autistic features", whether they fitted Kanner's or Asperger's descriptions or had bits and pieces of both, had in common absence or impairments of social interaction, communication and development of imagination. They also had a narrow, rigid, repetitive pattern of activities and interests. The three impairments (referred to as the 'triad') were shown in a wide variety of ways, but the underlying similarities were recognizable.'

Slide 3

Mind-blindness (Baron-Cohen 1990; 1995)

- People with autism lack a 'theory of mind'.

- **Theory of mind** is the ability to appreciate the mental states of oneself and other people.

- It is a prerequisite to effective functioning in social groups.

- It is usually evident in children from around the age of 4 onwards.

- However, children with autism seem to lack the ability to 'think about thoughts' (Happe 1994).

Slide 4

Executive function (Norman and Shallice 1980)

- **Executive function** is the mechanism which enables us to move our attention from one activity or object to another flexibly and easily.

- It allows us to plan strategically, solve problems and set ourselves objectives.

- The absence of such a mechanism determines that

    1 all our actions are controlled by the environment in response to cues and stimuli, leading to apparently meaningless activity

    2 actions and behaviours compete for dominance in a disorganised and inconsistent manner leading to an inability to plan and execute goal generated behaviour.

- In a school setting, this emerges as

    1 highly distractible behaviour

    2 dependence upon ritual and routines

    3 an apparent disregard for the school timetable or the completion of tasks.

Slide 5

Central coherence theory (Frith 1989)

- Natural impulse to place information into a context in order to give it meaning.

- People with autism tend to focus on the detail rather than the whole.

- The failure to appreciate the whole accounts for the piecemeal way in which people with autism acquire knowledge and the unusual cognitive profile presented by many people with autism.

- Educators may detect the lack of central coherence in

  1 the narrowed interests of children with autism

  2 the ways in which students with autism are often unable to generalise skills

  3 the way in which children with autism often display areas of relative strength described as islets of ability.

Slide 6

Sensory processing

- We experience the world around us through seven sensory channels, namely

    1 Visual – what we see

    2 Auditory – what we hear

    3 Olfactory – what we smell

    4 Gustatory – what we taste

    5 Tactile – what we feel

    6 Vestibular – balance

    7 Proprioceptory – co-ordination.

- People with autism often experience difficulties in processing sensory stimuli.

- People with autism can be either hyper-sensitive (over-sensitive) or hypo-sensitive (under-sensitive) to specific stimuli.

- These difficulties can create a 'Gestalt perception' in which all stimuli are equally relevant.

- In order to regulate this difficulty people with autism may 'mono-process' sensory stimuli.

Slide 7

TEACCH

<u>T</u>reatment and <u>E</u>ducation of <u>A</u>utistic and related <u>C</u>ommunication handicapped <u>CH</u>ildren

- Lifelong programme for people with autism based on a recognition of characteristic strengths and typical impairments.

- Structured teaching has four major components

  1 Physical organisation

  2 Schedules

  3 Work systems

  4 Task organisation.

(Schopler and Mesibov 1995)

- Structured teaching can be incorporated into mainstream practice through use of the four major components.

(Mesibov and Howley 2003)

Slide 8

PECS

<u>P</u>icture <u>E</u>xchange <u>C</u>ommunication <u>S</u>ystem

- Picture provides permanence of information.

- Allows processing time which supports understanding.

- Learner initiates communicative acts.

- Takes the learner through six phases, namely

    1 Phase One – Initiating communication

    2 Phase Two – Expanding the use of pictures

    3 Phase Three – Choosing the message in PECS

    4 Phase Four – Introducing the sentence structure in PECS

    5 Phase Five – Teaching answering simple questions

    6 Phase Six – Teaching commenting.

(Bondy and Frost 2002)

- Appropriate for students with language as it supports comprehension and allows extension of existing skills.

References

American Psychiatric Association (1994) *Diagnostic and Statistical Manual of Mental Disorders – Fourth Edition.*Washington DC: American Psychiatric Association.

Asperger, H. (1944) 'Die autistichen psychopathen im kindesalter', *Archiv für Psychiatrie und Nervenkrankenheiten* (Autistic Psychopathy in Childhood), 117: 76–136.

Atwood, T. (1998) *Asperger's Syndrome: A Guide for Parents and Professionals.* London and Philadelphia, PA: Jessica Kingsley.

Baird, G., Simonoff, E., Pickles, A., Chandler, S., Loucas, T., Meldrum, T. and Charman, T. (2006) 'Prevalence of disorders of the autism spectrum in a population cohort of children in South Thames: The Special Needs and Autism Project (SNAP)', *The Lancet,* 368(9531): 179–81.

Baron-Cohen, S. (1990) 'Autism: a specific cognitive disorder of "mind-blindness"', *International Review of Psychiatry,* 2: 79–88.

Baron-Cohen, S. (1995) *Mindblindness: An Essay on Autism and Theory of Mind.* London: Bradford Books.

Bogdashina, O. (2003) *Sensory Perceptual Issues in Autism and Asperger Syndrome: Different Sensory Experiences, Different Perceptual Worlds.* London and Philadelphia, PA: Jessica Kingsley.

Bondy, A.S. and Frost, L. (2002) *A Picture's Worth: PECS and Other Visual Communication Strategies in Autism.* Bethesda, Washington, DC: Woodbine House.

Campbell, R., Baron-Cohen, S. and Walker, J. (1995) 'Do people with autism show a whole face advantage in recognition of familiar faces and their parts? A test of central coherence theory', unpublished manuscript, University of London, Goldsmith's College.

Charman, T. and Care, P. (2004) *Mapping Autism Research.* London: National Autistic Society.

Cohen, D. and Volkmar, F. (1997) *Handbook of Autism and Pervasive Developmental Disorders.* New York: John Wiley.

Cumine, V., Dunlop, J. and Stevenson, G. (2009) *Autism in the Early Years: Resource Materials for Teachers.* London: David Fulton.

Department for Education (DfE) (2011) *Support and Aspiration: A New Approach to Special Educational Needs and Disability.* London: HMSO.

Dunn, W. (2008) *Sensory Profile.* Harlow: Pearson Education.

Frith, U. (1989) *Autism: Explaining the Enigma*. Oxford: Blackwell.

Frost, L.A. and Bondy, A.S. (1994) *PECS: The Picture Exchange Communication System Training Manual*. Cherry Hill, NJ: Pyramid Educational Consultants.

Frost, L.A. and Bondy, A.S. (2002) *The Picture Exchange Communication System – Training Manual*. Newark, DE: Pyramid Educational Products.

Gillberg, C. (1985) 'Asperger's Syndrome and recurrent psychosis: a case study', *Journal of Autism and Developmental Disorders*, 15(4): 389–97.

Gorrod, L. (1997) *My Brother is Different: A Book for Children Who Have a Brother or Sister with Autism*. London: National Autistic Society.

Gray, C. (1994a) *The Social Story Book*. Arlington, TX: Future Horizons.

Gray, C. (1994b) *Comic Strip Conversations*. Arlington, TX: Future Horizons.

Gray, C. and Leigh White, A. (2002) *My Social Stories Book*. London: Jessica Kingsley.

Grandin, T. (1986) *Emergence Labelled Autistic*. New York: Warner Books.

Haddon, M. (2003) *The Curious Incident of the Dog in the Night-Time*. London: Vintage Books.

Hanbury, M. (2007) *Positive Behaviour Strategies to Support Children and Young People with Autism*. London, Thousand Oaks, CA and Delhi: SAGE.

Happe, F. (1994) *Autism: An Introduction to Psychological Theory*. London: UCL Press.

Howlin, P., Baron-Cohen, S. and Hadwin, J. (1999) *Teaching Children with Autism to Mind-Read: A Practical Guide*. Chichester: John Wiley.

Jordan, R. and Powell, S. (1995) *Understanding and Teaching Children with Autism*. Chichester: John Wiley.

Kanner, L. (1943) 'Autistic disturbances of affective contact', *The Nervous Child*, 2: 217–50.

Lawson, W. (2000) *Life Behind Glass: A Personal Account of Autism Spectrum Disorder*. London and Philadelphia, PA: Jessica Kingsley.

Leslie, A. M. (1987) 'Pretence and representation: the origins of "theory of mind"', *Psychological Review*, 94: 412–26.

Mesibov, G. and Howley, M. (2003) *Accessing the Curriculum for Pupils with Autistic Spectrum Disorders*. London: David Fulton.

Miller, L. (2009) *Practical Behaviour Management Solutions for Children and Teens with Autism: The 5P Approach*. London and Philadelphia, PA: Jessica Kingsley.

Morrison, K. (2002) *School Leadership and Complexity Theory*. London: RoutledgeFalmer.

Moyes, R.A. (2001) *Incorporating Social Goals in the Classroom: A Guide for Teachers and Parents of Children with High-Functioning Autism and Asperger's Syndrome*. London and Philadelphia, PA: Jessica Kingsley.

NIASA (2003) *National Autism Plan for Children*. London: National Autistic Society.

Nind, M. and Hewett, D. (1994) *Access to Communication: Developing the Basics of Communication with People with Severe Learning Difficulties through Intensive Interaction*. London: David Fulton.

Nind, M. and Hewett, D. (2001) *A Practical Guide to Intensive Interaction*. Kidderminster: BILD Publications.

Norman, D. and Shallice, T. (1980) 'Attention to action: willed and automatic control of behaviour', in R. Davidson, G. Schwartz and D. Shapiro (eds), *Consciousness and Selfregulation*. Vol. 4. New York: Plenum Press. pp. 1–18.

Lorenz, E.N. (1963) 'Deterministic non periodic flow', *Journal of the Atmospheric Sciences*. Vol. 20(2): 130–41.

Potter, C. and Whittaker, C. (2001) *Enabling Communication in Children with Autism*. London: Jessica Kingsley.

Prevezer, W. (1990) 'Strategies for tuning into autism', *Therapy Weekly*, 17(16), October.

Rimland, B. (1964) *Infantile Autism*. New York: Appleton-Century-Crofts.

Robinson, S. (2008) *Accredited Courses in Autism*. Kidderminster: BILD.

Sainsbury, C. (2009) *Martian in the Playground*. 2nd edition. London, Thousand Oaks, CA and New Delhi: SAGE.

Schopler, E. and Mesibov, G. (1995) *Learning and Cognition in Autism*. New York: Plenum Press.

Scott, F.J., Baron-Cohen, S., Bolton, P. and Brayne, C. (2002) 'The CAST (Childhood Asperger Syndrome Test): preliminary development of a UK screen for mainstream primary-school aged children', *Autism 2002*, 6: 9–31.

Shah, A. and Frith, U. (1983) 'An islet of ability in autism: a research note,' *Journal of Child Psychology and Psychiatry*, 34: 613–20.

Sherrat, D. and Peter, M. (2002) *Developing Play and Drama in Children with Autistic Spectrum Disorders*. London: David Fulton.

Sigman, M., Mundy, P., Ungerer, J. and Sherman, T. (1986) 'Social interactions of autistic, mentally retarded, and normal children and their caregivers', *Journal of Child Psychology and Psychiatry*, 27(5): 647–56.

Stock Kranowitz, C. (2003) *The Out-of-Sync Child Has Fun: Activities for Kids with Sensory Integration Dysfunction*. New York: Perigree.

Wall, K. (2010) *Autism and Early Years Practice*. 2nd edition. London, Thousand Oaks, CA and Delhi: SAGE.

Whitaker, P., Joy, H., Harley, J. and Edwards, D. (2001) *Challenging Behaviour and Autism: Making Sense – Making Progress*. London: National Autistic Society.

Williams, D. (1992) *Nobody Nowhere*. London and Philadelphia, PA: Jessica Kingsley.

Wimpory, D. (1995) 'Brief report: musical interaction therapy for children with autism: an evaluative case study', *Journal of Autism and Developmental Disorders*, 25(5): 541–52.

Wing, L. (1996) *The Autistic Spectrum*. London: Constable and Robinson.

Wing, L. and Gould, J. (1979) 'Severe impairments of social interaction and associated abnormalities in children: epidemiology and classification', *Journal of Autism and Childhood Schizophrenia*, 9: 11–29.

Wing, L. and Potter, D. (2002) 'The epidemiology of autistic spectrum disorders: is prevalence rising?', *Mental Retardation and Developmental Disabilities Research Reviews*, 8(3): 151–61.

World Health Organization (1993) *Mental Disorders: A Glossary and Guide to their Classification in Accordance with the 10th Revision of the International Classification of Diseases (ICD-10)*. Geneva: World Health Organization.

Index

Added to a page number 'f' denotes a figure.

A
accepting 38–9
accredited courses 30–1
achievement, recognising 35
acoustics 73
adaptations
  student-focused 72–3
  to the physical environment 73–4
adaptive behaviour 9
adaptive systems 98
adaptive thinking 18
adult-adult interaction (case study) 65
aggressive behaviour 22
'alert' stage 72
alternatives 51–2
American Psychiatric Association (APA) 6
anger, parental 23
anxiety, parental 23
appendix model (curriculum) 100, 102
approachability 31
Asperger, Hans 3, 4
Asperger's Syndrome 4, 5
aspiration, culture of 102
assessment
  communication profiles 63
  of learning needs
    clarity of purpose 76–7
    methods 78–80
    perspectives 77–8
  of sensory needs 71
  tools 79
  see also risk assessment
attitudes
  sharing positive 27–35
  to autism 23–5
autism
  addressing behavioural issues 37–54
  awareness of 13, 34, 56
  causation 5–6
  changing context 12–13
  developing the curriculum for 95–109
  diagnosis 6–7, 13
  effective and established strategies 75–94
  impact on learning 15–25
  Kanner and Asperger 3–4
  models of 8–12
  national approach 12
  prevalence 7–8

autism cont.
  relationship between Asperger's Syndrome and 5
  strategy for adults 12
Autism Act (2009) 12
Autism Cymru 12
Autism Education Trust 12
Autism Genome Project 6, 13
autism specific learning 104, 105, 108
awareness of autism 13, 34, 56

B
background noise 61
Baron-Cohen, Simon 59
behaviour support plans 52, 53f
behavioural issues 21–2
  addressing 37–54
body language 65
Bogdashina, Olga 11, 71
'bolt-on' curriculum 100, 102
Bondy, Andy 87
brain scan technology 13
British Institute of Learning Disability 54

C
'calming' stage 72
Carpenter, Barry 95
'cause and effect' teaching 97
celebrating 43
central coherence theory 10–11
centrally imposed curriculum projects 100
change
  helping to understand 68–9
  planning for 69–70
child-adult interaction (case study) 65
classrooms
  developing flexible thinking 67–71
  impact of autism in 15–25
  physical organisation/environment 73–4, 82–4
  social understanding in 55–62
  supporting communication 62–7
  supporting sensory processing 71–4
cognitive ability 59
coherent understanding 91
collaborative parents 24
collaborative planning 79–80
collaborative practice 108

comic strips 60
communication
    consistency in 58
    impairment 8, 9, 17
    interventions *see* interventions
    profiles, assessment 63
    of routines 56
    strategies (child's) 63
    supporting 62–7
    see also non-verbal communication
'communication enabling
    environments' 89
compensating skills 56
complex learners 95, 97, 100
complex learning difficulties and
    disabilities (CLDD) 96
Complex Learning Difficulties and
    Disabilities Research Project 95
complex systems 96, 98
complexity and learning 95, 96–8
complexity theory 96, 97f
consistency 52, 56, 58, 66
consultation 38, 43, 63, 64, 66
contact records 33
context, and assessment 77
context cues 10, 59
continuing professional development
    30–1
controlling unpredictability 56
curriculum
    for autism 95–109
    evaluation of provision 102, 103f
    see also National Curriculum
cynicism, parental 23

D
dangerous behaviour 84
Data Protection Act 80
defensiveness, parental 23
describing change 69
desensitisation 40–2
Design for autism 73
detail, focus on 10
developmental impairments 6, 10
*Diagnostic and Statistical Manual of Mental
    Conditions* (DSM III) 6
distraction techniques 41
distractions, minimising 61, 83
dividers 83
double helix curriculum model 102–8
'driving in neutral' 44–6
Dunn, Winnie 71
dynamic environments, inflexible thinking
    in 18

E
ear defenders 73
effect of emotional states, appreciating 59
elasticity in thinking 68

embedded figures, ability to find 10
emotions, interpreting 58–60
empathic awareness 59
enabled, to engage in play 92
English, double helix planning template
    105, 106f, 108
environment *see* communication-enabling
    environments; dynamic environments;
    learning environments; physical
    environment
environmental permanence 42
evaluation
    of interventions 93–4
    of practitioner work 75
events, unpredictability of 56
evolutionary processes 18
executive function 10
exercise breaks 72
expertise 27, 32, 96
explaining 39, 69
expression of emotion 59–60
eye contact 90

F
'failure to appreciate the whole' 11
familiarity, in communication 64
fear 21
    overcoming 37–43
    response 38
fight 22
finish boxes 86
first impressions 31
flexibility (curriculum) 101–2, 105
flexible thinking, developing 67–71, 84
flight responses 21–2
    addressing 43–7
Forst, Lori 87

G
gender bias 8
genetics 6, 8, 13
Gestalt perception 20
goal-generated behaviour 10
gradual introduction, to stressful
    experiences 40–1
Gray, Carol 92
grief, parental 23
guidance (task) 61

H
Hewett, Dave 89
holistic approach 98, 100, 105, 108
home-school relationships, nurturing
    31–2
honesty 32
Howley, Marie 86
humour 66
hyper-sensitive responses 11, 20
hypo-sensitive responses 11, 20

I
ideas, sharing 32
identification
   of behaviour 48
   of child's communication strategies 63
idioms 66
ill health 78
imagination impairment 8, 9, 10, 18
inappropriate behaviours 84
inclusion agenda 86
Inclusion Development Programme (IDP)
   25, 30
inclusive curriculum 100, 102–4
individual needs, understanding 34
infantile autism 6
inflexible thinking 18, 68
information permanence 88
information sharing 34, 80
informing 69
INSET days 30
INSET materials 112–21
Intensive Interaction 89–90
interaction, with sensitive adults 92
interaction skills 91
International Statistical Classification of
   Diseases and Related Health Problems
   (ICD 10) 6
interventions 75, 80–94
   effective 80
   evaluation 93–4
   important features 81
   integrating 80
   Intensive Interaction 89–90
   minimal speech approach 88–9
   musical interaction 90–1
   NACP cautions 80
   nutritional 13
   PECS 34, 87–8
   play-drama 91–2
   social stories 92–3
   SPELL 87
   TEACCH 34, 56, 81–7
   violent behaviour 47–51
investigation, task refusal 46
irregular learning profiles 77–8
isolationist parents 24

J
jigs 86
joint attention 10, 68, 90, 92

K
Kanner, Leo 3–4

L
language 58, 64, 88
Lawson, Wendy 11
learning
   autism specific 104, 105, 108
   complexity and 95, 96–8

learning cont.
   impact of autism on 15–25
   a structure for 100–2
learning environments 20, 74
learning landscape 77
learning needs
   assessment see assessment
   recognition of 87
learning profiles, irregular 77–8
light 73
low impact environmental adjustments 73
'low-level noise' approach 83

M
mathematics, double helix planning
   template 105, 107f, 108
Medical Research Council 13
mental attitude 10
Mesibov, Gary 86
micro-evaluative approach 100, 105
mind-blindness 9–10
Mindreading 59
minimal speech approach 88–9
modelling 42
mono-processing 11, 20
Morrison, Keith 97
motivated, to engage in play 92
MP3 players 73
musical interaction 90–1

N
National Autism Plan for Children 76
National Autistic Society 7–8, 12,
   66, 87
National Curriculum 86, 87, 100, 108
needs
   addressing 48, 49f, 50f
   and challenging behaviour 48
   see also individual needs; learning needs
neurology 5, 6
neutral approach 44–6
neutral materials 61
newness 77
Nind, Melanie 89
noise 83
non-verbal communication 17, 66
   see also body language; eye contact
nutritional interventions 13

O
observation, of communication
   63, 64
observation checklist 29f
obsession, dealing with 46–7
openness 24, 32, 66
'optimally stimulating' learning
   environments 74, 82
optimism, parental 23
'organisation' stage 72
Outreach 30

P

parent-baby interaction 89–90
parents
    attitudes to autism 23–4
    see also home-school relationships
PECS 34, 87–8
pedagogy 98–100
peer pressure, deflating 35
peer relationships 33–5
peers, attitudes to autism 24
people, unpredictability of 56
perceptive sympathy 16
performance variability 77
permanence 42, 88
perseverance 68
personal practice, predictability of 56
personalised approach 98–9, 105
pervasive developmental disorder 6
Peter, Melanie 91
phobia 19
phrase books 60
physical environment 82–4
    adaptations 73–4
pica 84
planning
    for change 69–70
    collaborative 79–80
    double helix curriculum 105–8
play 10, 18
play-drama intervention 91–2
playgrounds 19
positive attitudes 25, 27–35
Potter, Carol 89
predicting change 69
pretend play 10
proactive programmes 52
problem solving 70
process, social stories as 93
processing time 46, 60–2
product, social stories as 93
professional development
    accredited courses 30–1
    informal approaches 28
    INSET days 30
    observation checklist 29f
    Outreach 30
professional knowledge 27, 34
professionals
    attitudes to autism 25
    working with 27–31
progression 105–8
proprioceptory difficulties 73
'prosthetic' sensory supports 72–3
psychology 5, 6
purposeful play experiences 92

R

rationale (curriculum) 101
re-focusing strategies 62
reactive strategies 52

realism (curriculum) 102
recognition
    of achievement 35
    of emotion 59
records of contact 33
refusal, addressing 44–6
relevance (curriculum) 101
relevant points, focusing on 61
remedial curriculum 56
repertoire of behaviours 67
repertoire of expression 60
resources 31
review of progress 93
risk assessment 44, 45f
ritualistic behaviour 38
rooms, location of 84
routines 56, 58, 88–9
running away 44

S

schedules 82, 84–6
schizophrenia 4
schools 9, 10
    see also home-school relationships
science, double helix planning template
        105, 107f, 108
Scottish Society for Autism 12
screens 73
self-esteem 24, 91
self-regulation 72
sensitive adults, interaction with 92
sensory audit 71
sensory circuits 72
sensory experiences, key channels 19
sensory needs, assessment of 71
sensory processing
    difficulties 11, 18–21
    supporting 71–4
Sensory Profile 71
Sensory Profile Checklist Revised 71
sensory stimuli 82–4
sentence types, in social stories 93
shared meaning 92
sharing ideas 32
Sherrat, Dave 91
silence 62
situational clues, reliance on 88–9
skilling up 41–2
small steps, tasks presented as 61
smells 83–4
social impairment 4, 8, 9, 16–17
social interactions 4, 8, 24
social stories 60, 92–3
social timing 90–1
social understanding, in the classroom
        55–62
socialisation 9
sounds, introducing 42
specialised knowledge (child's) 68
speech and language therapy services 63

SPELL 87
structure
  in communication 64
  effective curriculum 101
structured teaching 81–7
student profiles 56, 57f
student-focused adaptations 72–3
study boxes 86
superior abilities 10, 11
Support and Aspiration (DfE) 108
support materials 46, 61–2
supporting
  communication 62–7
  sensory processing 71–4
  to overcome fear 42

T
tactile sensations 84
task organisation 86
task refusal 44–6
taste 84
TEACCH 34, 56, 81–7
technological approach 99–100
textbooks 61
theory of mind 9, 10
time, child's need for 61
tinted glasses 73
trans-disciplinary approach 99, 105
transition areas 82

transitions, consistency in 58
triad of impairments 8–9
triangulation 77
trust 32, 66
turn-taking 90

U
understanding emotion 59
unfamiliarity 77
unpredictability 56–8

V
variable performance 77
vestibular difficulties 73
video recordings 63
violent behaviour 47–51
visual cueing systems 66
visual materials 64
visual reminders 85

W
weighted jackets 73
well-being, and assessment 78
Whittaker, Chris 89
Williams, Donna 11
Wing, Lorna 8
withdrawal 4
work systems 86
worksheets 61

THE INTENSIVE INTERACTION HANDBOOK

Dave Hewett *Independent Education Consultant and Author,* **Mark Barber** *Independent Education Consultant,* **Graham Firth** *Intensive Interaction Project Leader for Leeds Partnerships NHS Trust* and **Tandy Harrison** *Special Needs Teacher, Intensive Interaction Coordinator and parent*

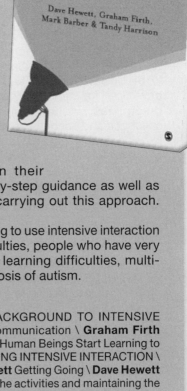

Intensive interaction is an approach to teaching the pre-speech fundamentals of communication to children and adults who have severe learning difficulties or autism, and who are still at an early stage of communication development. This book is a practical guide to help those wishing to implement intensive interaction in their setting, and it provides detailed advice and step-by-step guidance as well as a consideration of all the issues associated with carrying out this approach.

This book is a straightforward guide for anyone wanting to use intensive interaction with people with severe and complex learning difficulties, people who have very severe learning difficulties, profound and multiple learning difficulties, multi-sensory impairments, and people who have a diagnosis of autism.

CONTENTS
PART ONE: HUMAN COMMUNICATION AND THE BACKGROUND TO INTENSIVE INTERACTION \ **Dave Hewett** The Nature of Human Communication \ **Graham Firth** Background to Intensive Interaction \ **Dave Hewett** How Do Human Beings Start Learning to Communicate? \ PART TWO: THE PRACTICALITIES OF DOING INTENSIVE INTERACTION \ **Dave Hewett** Preparing for Intensive Interaction \ **Dave Hewett** Getting Going \ **Dave Hewett** Further and Continuing Progress \ **Mark Barber** Recording the activities and maintaining the processes \ **Graham Firth & Dave Hewett** Supporting Intensive Interaction in workplaces \ **Tandy Harrison** Doing Intensive Interaction at Home \ PART THREE: ISSUES, TOPICS AND COMMUNITY \ **Dave Hewett** Some associated Issues and Topics \ **Graham Firth** The Intensive Interaction Community \ Bibliography

READERSHIP
Special Needs professionals and for anyone interested in using intensive interaction with individuals with special needs

October 2011 • 168 pages
Cloth (978-0-85702-490-9) • £75.00
Paper (978-0-85702-491-6) • £24.99

ALSO FROM SAGE

YOUR DISSERTATION IN EDUCATION

Nicholas Walliman *Oxford Brookes University* and
Scott Buckler *University of Worcester*

Your Dissertation in Education provides a systematic, practical approach to dissertation and project writing for students in education. This is a revised edition of Nicholas Walliman's best-selling **Your Undergraduate Dissertation**, specifically developed for students from a range of educational disciplines, including teacher training, early childhood and education studies. This book is unique in being the first devoted to providing a complete overview of the dissertation process for education students.

Throughout the book use of practical examples, summary sections and additional references provide the reader with a comprehensive yet easy-to-read guide to ensure successful completion.

CONTENTS

PART I: INTRODUCTION TO THE DISSERTATION PROCESS \ What is a Dissertation? \ What is Educational Research? \ What's all this about Ethics? \ PART II: ESTABLISHING A FOCUS \ What will it be About? \ How do I Get Started? \ How do I Write a Proposal? \ How do I Write an Introduction? \ PART III: EXPLORING THE BACKGROUND TO THE TOPIC \ Where Do I Get Hold of all The Necessary Background Information? \ How Can I Manage all The Notes? \ What about Referencing? \ How do I Argue My Point Effectively? \ How do I Write a Literature Review? \ PART IV: CONDUCTING THE RESEARCH \ What Sorts of Data Will I Find and How Much do I Need? \ What's all this about Philosophy? \ How do I Conduct Effective Interviews? \ How do I Structure Effective Questionnaires? \ How do I Undertake Effective Observations? \ How do I Write a Methodology Chapter? \ PART V: ANALYZING THE DATA AND IDENTIFYING CONCLUSIONS \ How do I Analyze Quantitative Data? \ How do I Analyze Qualitative Data? \ How do I Write a Discussion Chapter? \ PART VI: PRACTICAL GUIDANCE ON THE SUBJECT \ How can I Work Effectively with My Supervisor? \ What about Working and Planning My Time? \ How can I Manage a Long Piece of Writing? \ How can I Make my Work Look Interesting and Easy to Read? \ How do I Cope With Stress? \ Who Else Might be Interested in My Writing?

SAGE STUDY SKILLS SERIES

2008 • 328 pages
Cloth (978-1-4129-4622-3) • £66.00 / Paper (978-1-4129-4623-0) • £17.99

ALSO FROM SAGE